Foreword

The future isn't coming; it's already here, reshaping the very fabric of our professional lives with an intensity few have truly grasped. "Unlock AI Skills That Will Make You Unstoppable by 2030," from Lucid Node Publishers, is not just a book—it's a survival guide for the impending AI revolution.

In these pages, you won't find theoretical musings or abstract predictions. Instead, you'll embark on a journey through the stark realities of our rapidly evolving landscape. The first chapter, "Extinction Event," confronts us with the uncomfortable truth: the AI revolution is not a gentle evolution but a seismic shift that will render many traditional jobs obsolete.

Yet, amidst this potential upheaval, lies an extraordinary opportunity. This book illuminates the path to not just surviving, but thriving. "Digital Darwinism" introduces the concept of the agile generalist, a vital archetype in an age where adaptability trumps specialization. You'll discover how to become a "One-Person Army," harnessing AI tools to emulate the polymathic brilliance of a Leonardo da Vinci.

The chapters that follow are a masterclass in practical application. "Code Without Coding" demystifies software development, empowering you to build with language, not just lines of code. "Your Digital Workforce" reveals how to create AI agents that work tirelessly, allowing you to scale your productivity exponentially. "The Creative Alchemist" transforms you into a content creation powerhouse, turning simple prompts into professional-grade output.

But this book isn't just about mastering individual tools. It's about strategic integration. "Influence Amplified" teaches you to build your brand in the AI era, while "The Force Multiplier" shows you how to combine AI powers for exponential results.

"Zero to Hero" provides a clear, actionable 90-day roadmap to AI mastery, ensuring you're not just reading about the future, but actively shaping it.

1

And as we peer "Beyond 2030," you'll gain the foresight to position yourself at the cutting edge of AI innovation.

In an era where change is the only constant, "Unlock AI Skills That Will Make You Unstoppable by 2030" is your essential companion. This book is a call to action, a blueprint for those ready to embrace the future and emerge not just unscathed, but utterly unstoppable.

Prepare to transform your career, your capabilities, and your very understanding of what's possible. The future is here. Are you ready?

Lucid Node Publishers

Table Of Contents

- Extinction Event: Why 50% of Jobs Won't Survive the AI Revolution
- Digital Darwinism: How Generalists Will Outcompete Specialists in the AI Age
- The One-Person Army: Becoming a Leonardo da Vinci with AI Tools
- Code Without Coding: Building Software with Your Words, Not Your Keyboard
- Your Digital Workforce: Creating AI Agents That Work While You Sleep
- The Creative Alchemist: Turning Prompts into Professional-Grade Content
- Influence Amplified: Building Your Audience and Brand in the AI Era
- The Force Multiplier: How to Combine AI Powers for Exponential Results
- Zero to Hero: The 90-Day Roadmap to AI Mastery
- Beyond 2030: Positioning Yourself for the Next Wave of AI Innovation

Chapter 1 : Extinction Event: Why 50% of Jobs Won't Survive the AI Revolution

The email arrived on a Tuesday morning. Sarah, a legal assistant at Johnson & Partners for eight years, opened it with her morning coffee. By the time she finished reading, the coffee had gone cold. The firm was implementing a new AI system that could review contracts in seconds. Her position— along with those of eleven colleagues—would be eliminated by the end of the month.

This scene is playing out across every industry, in companies of all sizes, around the world. It's not science fiction. It's happening right now.

Three floors down in the same building, Michael, a graphic designer with fifteen years of experience, was putting final touches on a branding package that had taken him three weeks to create. His phone buzzed with a notification. A competitor had just delivered a similar package to another client—created entirely with AI in less than a day, at one-tenth the cost. Michael's calendar showed no upcoming projects after this one.

Across town, Dr. Patel reviewed an X-ray, searching for signs of pneumonia. She'd spent twelve years in medical training to develop this skill. Meanwhile, at a nearby hospital, an AI system reviewed 500 similar X-rays in the time it took her to analyze one, with a higher detection rate and fewer false positives.

These aren't isolated incidents. They're early warning signs of a seismic shift that will reshape our economy and society more dramatically than any technological revolution in human history.

The Numbers Don't Lie

Let's get concrete about what we're facing. According to McKinsey's 2023 research, AI could automate up to 50% of current work activities by 2030. That's not 50% of some distant future jobs—that's half of the work being done today.

Bain's analysis paints an even bleaker picture: up to 80% of workers will face wage stagnation or displacement by 2030 due to AI and automation.

The World Economic Forum's Future of Jobs Report estimates that 85 million jobs may be displaced by the shift in labor division between humans and machines by 2025, while 97 million new roles may emerge. That sounds promising until you realize those new roles will require entirely different skills, and the transition will be anything but smooth.

This isn't just another technological shift. This is different. This is bigger.

We've Been Here Before (Sort Of)

To understand what's happening, let's look back at the Industrial Revolution. Beginning in the late 18th century, mechanical production fundamentally transformed society. Hand production gave way to steam-powered machines. Factories replaced workshops. Cities swelled as rural workers migrated for factory jobs.

Consider the textile industry. In 1800, weaving was done by skilled artisans who had trained for years. By 1850, power looms operated by unskilled workers had decimated this profession. A power loom could produce cloth 40 times faster than a skilled weaver. The weavers didn't just face wage cuts—they faced extinction.

In 1811, in Nottingham, England, a group of weavers gathered at night. Their livelihoods destroyed by mechanization, they began smashing the machines that had replaced them. These Luddites, as they came to be known, weren't technophobes. They were skilled workers fighting desperately for survival in a rapidly changing economy.

The British government's response? They deployed 12,000 troops to crush the rebellion—more soldiers than they had fighting Napoleon in Spain at the time. Parliament passed the Frame Breaking Act, making machine destruction punishable by death. Between 1811 and 1816, dozens of Luddites were hanged or transported to penal colonies.

The Industrial Revolution eventually created more jobs than it destroyed. Agricultural workers became factory laborers. New industries emerged. Standards of living ultimately rose. But this took decades, and the transition was brutal for many workers. Entire professions disappeared. New ones emerged. The economy transformed.

But here's the key difference with AI: the pace of change.

This Time Is Different

The Industrial Revolution unfolded over many decades. Steam engines were adopted gradually. Technical limitations slowed implementation. Workers had time—not much, but some—to adapt.

The Second Industrial Revolution in the late 19th century brought electricity, assembly lines, and mass production. Again, adoption was measured in decades.

The Digital Revolution of the late 20th century computerized offices and factories. Even then, changes occurred over years, not months.

AI capabilities are doubling approximately every six months. What was impossible last year is commonplace today. What seems far-fetched today will be routine tomorrow.

In 2015, AI systems struggled to reliably identify objects in images. By 2020, they could generate photorealistic images from text descriptions. By 2022, they could create professional-quality artwork, videos, and music. By 2023, they could write college-level essays, functional software code, and pass bar exams.

Let me share some concrete examples:

Radiologists: After 13 years of education and training, these medical specialists earn around $400,000 annually interpreting medical images. In 2023, Stanford researchers demonstrated an AI system that outperformed radiologists in detecting lung cancer from CT scans. The AI didn't just match human performance—it exceeded it. Google's DeepMind developed an AI that detected breast cancer from mammograms with greater accuracy than human radiologists, reducing false positives by 5.7% and false negatives by 9.4%. For a profession centered entirely on image interpretation, these advances aren't just threatening—they're existential.

Paralegals: These legal professionals spend years learning to review contracts and prepare legal documents. JPMorgan's COIN software now accomplishes in seconds what used to take legal aides 360,000 hours annually. One program, 360,000 hours eliminated. Harvey AI, a legal-specific large language model, is already being used by law firms like Allen & Overy to review documents, draft contracts, and perform legal research. In a test, lawyers using Harvey completed tasks 73% faster than those working without AI assistance.

Customer Service Representatives: Call centers worldwide employ millions. Yet companies like Air Canada, United Airlines, and PayPal are already deploying AI customer service systems that can handle complex queries, understand multiple languages, and operate 24/7 without breaks. Google's Duplex AI can make phone calls to schedule appointments, speaking so naturally that humans on the other end can't tell they're talking to an AI. Amelia, an AI platform from IPsoft, handles customer service for companies like Shell, Allstate, and Becton Dickinson, resolving up to 70% of queries without human intervention.

Content Writers: Journalists, copywriters, and technical writers face AI that can produce articles, product descriptions, and reports at a fraction of the cost. Bloomberg already uses AI to write financial reports. Associated Press employs AI for sports coverage and business news. The Guardian has published articles written entirely by AI. Jasper, an AI writing platform, serves over 50,000 paying business customers who use it to generate marketing copy, blog posts, and social media content.

Software Developers: Even coding itself—the skill that built the digital age—isn't safe. GitHub Copilot can write functional code from simple English descriptions. DeepMind's AlphaCode can solve competitive programming problems at the level of an average human programmer. When AI systems can write their own code, debug it, and improve it, the very people building AI tools may find themselves replaced by them.

Financial Analysts: Wall Street analysts spend years mastering financial modeling and market analysis. Now, AI systems from firms like Two Sigma and Renaissance Technologies not only analyze market data but make trading decisions faster and more effectively than human traders. BlackRock's Aladdin AI platform manages risk analysis for $21.6 trillion in assets—roughly 7% of the world's financial assets. JPMorgan's LOXM AI executes trades with far greater efficiency than human traders.

Middle Management: Managers who primarily coordinate work, track performance, and ensure compliance face particular risk. AI systems can monitor productivity, optimize scheduling, and enforce standards more consistently and at lower cost than human managers. Amazon already uses algorithms to track warehouse worker productivity and automatically generate warnings or terminations for underperformance, with minimal human oversight.

Transportation Workers: The 3.5 million truck drivers in the United States face eventual displacement from autonomous vehicles. While full autonomy has taken longer than some predicted, steady progress continues. Aurora, Waymo, TuSimple, and other companies are already conducting autonomous trucking trials on public roads. Once the technology matures, the economic incentive for adoption will be overwhelming: trucks that can operate 24/7 without rest periods or salary requirements.

The Extinction Pattern

When environments change gradually, species adapt. When changes occur suddenly, mass extinctions follow. The dinosaurs dominated Earth for 165 million years—until an asteroid impact changed their environment overnight. They had no time to adapt.

The business world has its own dinosaurs: companies that once seemed invincible but failed to adapt to technological change. Kodak invented digital photography but clung to film. Blockbuster passed on the chance to buy Netflix for $50 million. Nokia dominated mobile phones but missed the smartphone revolution.

What happened to these companies is now happening to entire professions. The asteroid has hit. The dust cloud is rising. And unlike the Industrial Revolution, we won't have decades to adapt.

Consider the secretarial profession. In 1980, the United States had 2.1 million secretaries. The personal computer and office software transformed this role. Today, executives who once relied on secretaries for correspondence, scheduling, and filing now handle much of this work themselves using digital tools. The number of traditional secretaries has declined by over 65%, and the role has fundamentally changed for those who remain.

This transformation took 40 years. The AI revolution will compress similar changes into less than a decade.

A Two-Tier Economy Emerges

As AI capabilities expand, a new economic reality is taking shape—a two-tier economy.

In the upper tier: those who can harness AI. These individuals will experience unprecedented productivity and earning power. They'll leverage AI to amplify their capabilities, automating routine work while focusing on high-value tasks. A single person with the right AI tools can now accomplish what previously required an entire team or department.

In the lower tier: those replaced by AI. These workers will face persistent wage pressure, job insecurity, and cycles of retraining for positions that themselves become automated shortly after. They'll compete for roles in sectors temporarily resistant to automation—until those sectors, too, are transformed by increasingly capable AI systems.

The gap between these tiers won't just be large—it will be unprecedentedly massive. History shows that technological revolutions initially increase inequality before new systems evolve to distribute gains more widely. But that redistribution isn't automatic—it requires intentional adaptation.

Think of the wealth gap between tech billionaires and average workers today. Now imagine that gap replicated across the entire economy, with AI-empowered individuals and organizations capturing ever-larger portions of economic value, while others struggle to find stable footing in a constantly shifting landscape.

The Fallout Has Already Begun

The early tremors of this economic earthquake are already visible:

In May 2023, IBM announced plans to pause hiring for roles that could potentially be replaced by AI, affecting approximately 7,800 positions. CEO Arvind Krishna predicted that 30% of non-customer-facing roles could be replaced by AI and automation within five years.

In January 2023, Microsoft laid off 10,000 employees, many in teams that could be augmented or replaced by AI capabilities. CEO Satya Nadella explicitly linked the layoffs to investment in AI, stating the company was "allocating both our capital and talent to areas of secular growth and long-term competitiveness for the company."

Beyond tech giants, marketing agencies, financial services firms, and media companies are quietly replacing entry-level creative and analytical roles with AI systems. A Boston Consulting Group study found that managers using AI completed tasks 40% faster and delivered 40% higher quality output compared to those without AI assistance. When a single person with AI can do the work of two people without it, staffing decisions become obvious.

The casualties aren't limited to low-skilled workers. Highly educated professionals in law, medicine, finance, and design—people who invested years in specialized training and graduate degrees—are finding their expertise challenged by systems that can perform core aspects of their work with comparable or superior results.

Widespread Economic Disruption

The broader economic implications are staggering. A 2023 Goldman Sachs report estimates that generative AI could drive annual GDP growth of 1.5% over a ten-year period and ultimately automate tasks worth $7 trillion in current labor costs. The same report predicts that generative AI could expose the equivalent of 300 million full-time jobs to automation.

These aren't just shifts within existing economic structures—they represent a fundamental restructuring of how value is created and distributed. As AI systems become more capable, they'll capture an increasing share of tasks currently performed by humans across virtually every industry.

Consider manufacturing, where automation has been a factor for decades. Traditional automation required significant capital investment, operated in structured environments, and could only perform specific, pre-programmed tasks. Modern AI-powered robotics systems can learn new tasks through demonstration, adapt to variable conditions, and work alongside humans in unstructured environments. Companies like Fetch Robotics and Boston Dynamics are already deploying such systems in warehouses and factories.

In retail, Amazon Go stores operate without cashiers, using computer vision and sensor fusion to track what customers take from shelves and automatically charge their accounts. Walmart has expanded its use of inventory robots and self-checkout systems. As these technologies mature and costs decrease, the 15.8 million Americans employed in retail face major disruption.

Even creative fields are not immune. DALL-E, Midjourney, and Stable Diffusion generate original artwork from text descriptions. RunwayML creates videos from text prompts. Jukebox produces original music in specific styles. While creative professionals may adapt by using these tools, they'll need fewer assistants and junior staff, shrinking the entry points to these careers.

The Path Forward

There's a natural reaction to this scenario: fear. Fear leads to denial or paralysis. Neither will save your career.

The path forward isn't to resist change but to position yourself on the right side of it. This doesn't mean becoming a coding expert or AI researcher. Those specialized roles themselves face disruption as AI systems become capable of designing and improving themselves.

The winners in this new economy will be those who become AI generalists—individuals who can leverage artificial intelligence across multiple domains to become extraordinarily capable and adaptable.

In 2023, OpenAI CEO Sam Altman noted that his tech CEO friends were taking bets on when we'd see the first one-person billion-dollar company. Not 10-person, not 5-person—one person, with AI handling tasks that once required entire departments.

This isn't hyperbole. Consider Jake Nichols, who operates Beehiiv, a newsletter platform serving thousands of customers with just five employees. Or Pieter Levels, who built and runs multiple million-dollar businesses as a solo entrepreneur using automation and AI tools. These pioneers show what's possible when one person can harness AI to multiply their capabilities.

From Specialization to Generalization

For decades, career advisors have urged specialization. "Go deep in one area," they said. "Become the expert. Make yourself irreplaceable."

This strategy worked in a stable environment where knowledge and skills evolved gradually. It fails in an environment of rapid, discontinuous change—especially when AI systems can rapidly acquire specialized knowledge.

In the AI era, the most valuable professionals won't be specialists with deep knowledge in one domain. They'll be generalists who can work across domains, leveraging AI tools to access specialized capabilities as needed.

Consider evolutionary biology: In stable environments, specialized species thrive by exploiting specific niches. The giant panda evolved to eat only bamboo, with a specialized thumb for stripping bamboo leaves. This works perfectly—until the bamboo forest faces disruption.

In contrast, generalists like raccoons can eat almost anything and adapt to diverse habitats. When environments change dramatically, these adaptable generalists survive and thrive while specialists face extinction.

The professional world is experiencing its own version of environmental upheaval. The specialized pandas—radiologists who can only read images, paralegals who can only review contracts, copywriters who can only write marketing materials—face existential threat. The adaptable raccoons— professionals who can work across disciplines, quickly learn new tools, and combine human judgment with AI capabilities—will flourish.

Becoming an AI Generalist

The AI generalist isn't just someone who uses AI tools. They're individuals who strategically combine AI capabilities across multiple domains to become extraordinarily productive and adaptable.

While specialists might achieve peak performance in narrow domains through years of dedicated practice, AI generalists can rapidly achieve 80- 90% of specialist-level capabilities across multiple domains simultaneously. They might not match the absolute pinnacle of human specialist performance, but they can operate at professional levels across diverse areas with far less time investment.

This isn't merely about efficiency—it's about becoming capable of work that was previously impossible for any individual. An AI generalist can design products, write marketing copy, build websites, analyze data, produce videos, manage customer support, and handle legal compliance— roles that traditionally required entire teams working together.

This isn't a distant possibility. It's happening now. In the chapters that follow, I'll show you exactly how to become that one-person army—that AI generalist who thrives while others struggle to survive.

The Alternative Is Grim

Those who fail to adapt face a challenging future. As routine cognitive work is automated, those without AI skills will compete for a shrinking pool of jobs that still require human touch but minimal technical expertise—roles in personal care, service, and human interaction.

These roles typically offer lower wages, less security, and fewer advancement opportunities. The competition for such positions will intensify as displaced workers from automated sectors seek refuge in these temporarily protected domains.

Meanwhile, those who master AI tools will experience unprecedented leverage, accomplishing more with less effort and fewer resources. The productivity gap between AI-empowered individuals and traditional workers will widen exponentially, creating economic disparities that dwarf today's inequality.

Beyond Economics: Identity and Meaning

The disruption extends beyond economics to questions of identity and purpose. Many professionals define themselves through their work. When AI can perform their specialized skills—often better than they can—it challenges not just their livelihood but their sense of self-worth and social value.

A radiologist who spent 13 years training to interpret medical images must confront a profound question: What value do I provide in a world where an AI can do my core task more accurately? Similar existential questions face writers, artists, programmers, and countless other professionals whose identity is tied to skills now replicable by machines.

This psychological dimension of the AI revolution may prove as challenging as the economic one. Those who survive and thrive won't just need new skills—they'll need new frameworks for deriving meaning and identity in a world where uniquely human capabilities take center stage.

Looking Ahead: The Ultimate Advantage

The job market extinction event is underway. But unlike the dinosaurs, we can see the asteroid coming. We can adapt. And those who do won't just survive—they'll thrive in ways previously unimaginable.

In 1997, when IBM's Deep Blue defeated world chess champion Garry Kasparov, many predicted the end of human chess. Instead, a new form emerged: centaur chess, where human-AI teams compete. These centaurs—humans working with AI assistance—consistently outperform both solo humans and solo AI systems.

This centaur model points to our future across all domains. The ultimate competitive advantage won't belong to pure AI systems or to unaugmented humans. It will belong to AI generalists—humans who can effectively partner with artificial intelligence, directing and harnessing its capabilities while contributing distinctly human elements: creativity, empathy, ethical judgment, and contextual understanding.

The question isn't whether AI will transform your career. The question is whether you'll be Sarah, receiving that devastating email, or whether you'll be the person who sent it—perhaps while simultaneously running three other businesses from your laptop.

The choice is yours. In the following chapters, I'll show you exactly how to master the eight essential AI skills that will make you unstoppable in 2030 and beyond. We'll start with the Power to Build—creating software without knowing how to code—in Chapter 2, and then progress through each fundamental power needed to thrive in the AI age.

The future belongs to those who prepare for it today. Let's get started.

Chapter 2: Digital Darwinism: How Generalists Will Outcompete Specialists in the AI Age

The Great Reversal

For most of the 20th century, the career advice remained remarkably consistent: specialize. Go deep into one field. Become the expert. The safest path to prosperity was to pick a lane and stay in it for decades. Radiologists dedicated a decade to mastering medical imaging. Corporate lawyers spent seven years perfecting contract law. Software developers devoted years to mastering specific programming languages.

And it worked. Specialization was the winning strategy in a stable economy. But what happens when stability disappears?

We're witnessing a complete reversal of this fundamental career equation. As AI systems begin matching or exceeding specialist performance across countless domains, the specialist advantage is rapidly eroding.

Consider what's happened to radiologists. After investing a decade in training, many now find themselves collaborating with AI systems that can detect certain cancers with equal or greater accuracy. A 2023 study published in *The Lancet Digital Health* found that AI outperformed radiologists in detecting breast cancer in screening mammograms by 11.5%.

Legal document review, once the bread and butter of junior associates billing $300 per hour, can now be performed by AI systems in minutes rather than hours. The legal AI platform Harvey can analyze contracts and produce summaries faster than human lawyers while catching details humans might miss.

As one New York attorney confided to me, "I spent my life becoming an expert in contract law. Now GPT-4 can draft better contracts than most of the partners at my firm in seconds."

The specialist career path has never been more vulnerable.

Nature's Lesson: Adapt or Die

To understand why AI is creating this reversal, we need to look at evolutionary biology's most important lesson.

Charles Darwin didn't actually coin the phrase "survival of the fittest" (that was Herbert Spencer), but Darwin's central insight remains profound: "It is not the strongest of the species that survives, nor the most intelligent. It is the one most adaptable to change."

Nature offers two primary adaptation strategies: specialization and generalization.

The Panda Problem

Consider the giant panda. Over millions of years, it evolved to eat almost exclusively bamboo. Its digestive system, teeth, and even its unique "thumb" (actually a modified wrist bone) are specialized adaptations for processing bamboo.

In stable times, this specialization serves the panda well. With limited competition for its food source, the panda thrived for millions of years.

But what happens when that stability is disrupted? When bamboo forests decline due to climate change or human development, pandas face extinction because they can't adapt to other food sources. Their specialization becomes their vulnerability.

The Raccoon Resilience

In contrast, raccoons are quintessential generalists. They can eat almost anything from insects and fruits to garbage and pet food. They adapt to urban, suburban, and rural environments. They're excellent climbers, swimmers, and problem solvers.

When humans transformed natural habitats into cities, many specialized species disappeared. But raccoons? They thrived. Their adaptability turned our trash cans into their buffets and our attics into their condos.

While pandas require massive conservation efforts to survive modest environmental changes, raccoons adapt and flourish amid radical transformations of their habitat.

The K-T Boundary of Careers

The most dramatic example of the specialist-generalist dynamic played out 66 million years ago when an asteroid struck Earth, causing the Cretaceous-Paleogene (K-Pg) extinction event.

The highly specialized dinosaurs—magnificent creatures perfectly adapted to their ecological niches—were wiped out. The T. Rex, with its specialized hunting adaptations, the pterosaurs with their specialized flight capabilities, and the marine reptiles with their specialized aquatic adaptations all disappeared.

Who survived? Small, unimpressive mammalian generalists—our ancient ancestors—who could eat anything, live anywhere, and quickly adapt to changing conditions.

We're witnessing a similar extinction-level event in the job market right now. The asteroid has a name: artificial intelligence.

The AI Asteroid: Why Specialists Are Vulnerable

The vulnerability of specialists in the AI age stems from three fundamental factors:

1. Replicability of Narrow Expertise

The more well-defined and rule-based a specialty is, the easier it is for AI to replicate. AI excels at tasks with clear parameters and abundant training data—precisely the conditions that define many specialized professions.

Take tax preparation. For decades, being a tax specialist meant job security. Today, AI-powered software like TurboTax handles millions of returns with increasing sophistication each year. The most straightforward tax preparation work is already being automated, leaving human tax preparers scrambling to justify their fees.

2. The Data Advantage

Specialists often pride themselves on their accumulated knowledge and experience. A veteran radiologist might boast of having seen 100,000 chest X-rays over a 30-year career.

But AI systems can be trained on millions of X-rays in weeks. They don't forget, don't get tired, and can identify patterns across datasets no human could comprehend. The human specialist's primary advantage—accumulated experience—is precisely what AI can scale beyond human capability.

A cardiologist at the Mayo Clinic recently told me, "I used to think my 30 years of experience reading EKGs made me irreplaceable. Now I'm watching an AI system that's been trained on 10 million EKGs outperform our department's best doctors."

3. The Scale Problem

Specialists often command high fees because of their scarcity. There are only so many world-class cardiac surgeons or elite intellectual property attorneys.

But once an AI system masters a specialty, it can scale infinitely at minimal cost. The knowledge that once resided in the minds of a few thousand specialists can now be deployed globally, 24/7, at a fraction of the cost.

This doesn't mean specialists will disappear overnight. But it does mean their economic value will face unprecedented pressure as AI democratizes access to their expertise.

The Rise of the AI Generalist

If specialists are the pandas of our professional ecosystem, AI generalists are the raccoons—adaptable, resilient, and poised to thrive amid disruption.

What exactly is an AI generalist? They're individuals who leverage AI tools to rapidly acquire capabilities across multiple domains that previously would have required years of specialized training.

The AI generalist might not match the peak performance of true specialists in every domain, but they can achieve 80-90% of specialist capabilities across multiple areas simultaneously. This creates a combined value proposition that no individual specialist can match.

Case Study: The Modern Marketing Department of One

Consider Sarah, a marketing consultant I worked with last year. Before embracing AI tools, she was a social media specialist who struggled to command fees beyond $50 per hour. Clients constantly questioned her value as social platforms changed algorithms and new channels emerged.

After becoming an AI generalist, Sarah transformed into a full-service marketing department. Using AI tools, she now:

- Creates professional-grade graphic designs with Midjourney and DALL-E 3
- Produces and edits client videos with Runway and Descript
- Builds simple marketing automation tools with no-code platforms
- Drafts SEO-optimized website copy with Claude and GPT-4
- Analyzes market research data using augmented analysis tools
- Creates custom marketing dashboards for clients

Sarah now charges $250 per hour as a marketing generalist, with a waitlist of clients. She delivers work that previously would have required a team of 5-7 specialists, each charging $75-150 per hour.

"Before AI, I was competing with thousands of social media specialists globally," Sarah told me. "Now I'm offering a combination of services that's unique to me and my workflow. Clients aren't hiring me for any one skill—

they're hiring me because I can do it all while maintaining a consistent vision."

Case Study: The Developer Who Doesn't Code (Much)

Michael was a mid-level JavaScript developer earning $120,000 at a tech company. Despite a decade in the field, he found himself competing with younger developers willing to work for less, and increasingly, competing with AI coding tools.

Rather than doubling down on JavaScript expertise, Michael pivoted to become an AI generalist. He now:

- Builds complete web applications by directing AI coding assistants
- Creates custom internal tools for businesses using AI-assisted development
- Designs UI/UX mockups with AI design tools
- Develops content strategies for apps using AI analysis
- Implements marketing automation for product launches
- Handles data analysis and visualization that would previously require a data scientist

Michael now runs a "technical solutions" consultancy charging $20,000 per project for work that would traditionally require a team of 3-4 specialists. His competitive advantage isn't deep expertise in any single area—it's his ability to deliver end-to-end solutions by orchestrating AI tools across multiple domains.

"I write maybe 20% of the code I used to," Michael explained. "But I deliver complete solutions instead of just code. My clients don't care how the work gets done—they care about results."

The Four Advantages of AI Generalists

The shift from human specialists to AI generalists is accelerating because generalists possess four distinct advantages in the AI economy:

1. Adaptability Advantage

When market conditions change, specialists often need years to retool their skills. AI generalists can pivot within weeks.

Consider the COVID-19 pandemic. When in-person events suddenly stopped, event planning specialists faced existential crisis. Meanwhile, digital generalists quickly adapted, using AI tools to create virtual event experiences, develop online community platforms, and implement digital engagement strategies.

The ability to rapidly acquire new capabilities through AI tools means generalists can surf the waves of disruption rather than being crushed by them.

2. Integration Advantage

The most valuable business problems rarely fit neatly within a single specialty. They exist at the intersection of multiple domains.

A company launching a new product doesn't need a marketing specialist, a design specialist, and a data analysis specialist working in isolation. They need integrated solutions that address the entirety of their challenge.

AI generalists excel at integration because they can bridge multiple domains, seeing connections that specialists miss. They're modern-day polymaths—renaissance thinkers for the digital age.

3. Innovation Advantage

Real innovation often happens at the boundaries between disciplines. When fields overlap, new possibilities emerge.

Specialists, focused deeply on their domain, often miss these boundary opportunities. AI generalists, working across multiple domains, naturally discover novel combinations and applications.

This is why some of history's greatest innovators were generalists. Leonardo da Vinci's genius stemmed from his ability to combine art, engineering, anatomy, and physics. The AI generalist follows in this tradition, using technology to achieve in weeks what might have taken da Vinci years to master.

4. Economic Advantage

Perhaps most importantly, AI generalists offer compelling economics. They can deliver 80-90% of the quality of multiple specialists at a fraction of the combined cost.

For many business needs, this "good enough" solution across multiple domains is more valuable than excellence in just one. A company with limited budget doesn't need a world-class graphic designer, a world-class copywriter, and a world-class web developer. They need a functional website that looks professional, communicates clearly, and works well.

The AI generalist delivers this complete solution at a price point no combination of specialists can match.

The New Professional Food Chain

As AI reshapes the professional landscape, a new hierarchy is emerging:

Tier 1: AI-Resistant Specialists (Temporary Safe Zone)

At the top remain a small number of truly elite specialists whose work involves elements AI cannot yet replicate—profound creativity, genuine human connection, or physical manipulation of the world.

World-class surgeons, elite therapists, and master craftspeople still command premium fees because their work combines specialized knowledge with physical skills or human elements that AI cannot fully replicate.

But this tier is shrinking as AI capabilities expand, and the economic premium these specialists command is under pressure.

Tier 2: AI Generalists (The New Winners)

The emerging professional elite are AI generalists who leverage technology to achieve specialist-level outputs across multiple domains.

These are the new renaissance professionals—individuals who might have been average performers in any single specialty but become extraordinary by combining 80-90% mastery across multiple domains.

Their competitive advantage lies not in being the best at any one thing, but in their ability to integrate across domains, adapt rapidly, and deliver complete solutions.

Tier 3: AI-Enhanced Specialists (The Transitional Majority)

Most specialists are evolving into AI-enhanced versions of their former selves. They use AI tools to augment their specialty but haven't yet expanded beyond their primary domain.

The AI-enhanced accountant uses AI for routine tax preparation but still focuses exclusively on financial services. The AI-enhanced graphic designer uses generative AI for initial concepts but still identifies primarily as a designer.

This tier represents a transitional state rather than a sustainable competitive position. As AI capabilities improve, the value of narrow specialization continues to decline.

Tier 4: Unaugmented Specialists (The Endangered Species)

At the bottom of the new hierarchy are specialists who resist AI augmentation entirely. They continue to practice their specialty using traditional methods, competing directly against increasingly capable AI systems.

The accountant who refuses to use AI-powered tax software, the translator who doesn't employ machine translation tools, the copywriter who dismisses AI writing assistants—all face a losing battle against technology that improves exponentially while their human capabilities remain relatively fixed.

Becoming an AI Generalist: The Path Forward

The strategic imperative is clear: to thrive in the AI age, you must become an AI generalist. But how?

The journey begins with mindset. You must let go of the specialist identity many of us were trained to develop. Instead of defining yourself by a single skill ("I'm a graphic designer," "I'm a programmer"), adopt a capability-focused identity: "I create solutions."

Next, you need to master the fundamental powers of the AI generalist:

1. **The Power to Build**: Creating software tools using AI-assisted development
2. **The Power to Automate**: Building AI agents and workflow automation systems
3. **The Power to Create**: Generating professional-grade content across mediums
4. **The Power to Connect**: Building influence and audience through AI-enhanced communication

These powers, working in concert, allow you to deliver value that was previously impossible for a single person to provide.

The good news? Unlike traditional skills that took years to master, AI-generalist capabilities can be acquired in months or even weeks using the right learning approach.

In the coming chapters, we'll explore each of these powers in detail, providing you with a clear roadmap to mastering the tools and techniques that will make you an unstoppable AI generalist.

The Choice: Adapt or Fade Away

The professional world is bifurcating into two groups: those who leverage AI to become extraordinarily capable generalists, and those who cling to traditional specialization while their economic value gradually erodes.

As Sam Altman, CEO of OpenAI, recently predicted, we're approaching an era where single individuals wielding AI tools will accomplish what previously required entire teams or companies. The "one-person billion-dollar company" is no longer a fantasy but an emerging possibility.

The parallels to biological evolution are striking. When environments change dramatically, specialists face extinction while generalists thrive. The career asteroid has hit. The question isn't whether the professional landscape will transform—it's whether you'll be among those who adapt and prosper in the new reality.

Darwin's insight has never been more relevant: in times of profound change, it is not the strongest or most intelligent who survive, but those most adaptable to change.

The choice is yours. Will you cling to specialization as your economic value gradually erodes? Or will you embrace the path of the AI generalist and position yourself at the forefront of the greatest transformation in human work since the Industrial Revolution?

Chapter 3: The One-Person Army: Becoming a Leonardo da Vinci with AI Tools

The Renaissance Reborn

In 15th century Florence, a young apprentice named Leonardo da Vinci began what would become one of history's most remarkable careers. By the time of his death, he had mastered painting, sculpture, architecture, engineering, anatomy, astronomy, botany, geology, and more—becoming the archetype of the Renaissance polymath.

What made da Vinci extraordinary wasn't just his mastery of individual domains but his ability to synthesize knowledge across disciplines. When he studied the flight of birds, it informed his aircraft designs. When he dissected human bodies, it enhanced his portraiture. His genius lay in connections that specialists, confined to their silos, could never perceive.

For centuries after da Vinci, such polymathic achievement became increasingly rare. The explosion of human knowledge made mastering multiple domains seem impossible. The educational and professional structures that emerged in the 20th century reinforced hyperspecialization, funneling individuals into narrower and narrower expertise.

But today, we stand at the dawn of a new Renaissance—a Digital Renaissance—where AI tools are democratizing expertise and making the generalist approach not just viable again, but advantageous.

The Digital Renaissance

Sam Altman, CEO of OpenAI, recently shared that among his tech CEO friends, they're taking bets on when we'll see the first one-person billion-dollar company—something previously unimaginable without AI. This isn't hyperbole; it's the logical conclusion of the force-multiplying capabilities AI puts at our fingertips.

Consider what da Vinci accomplished with quill, paper, and candlelight. Now imagine what he might have created with today's AI tools that can:

- Generate anatomically correct medical illustrations in seconds
- Simulate the physics of his flying machine designs
- Visualize architectural blueprints in 3D
- Translate his ideas into multiple languages
- Analyze data patterns across thousands of variables

What took da Vinci years to master, you can now leverage in weeks. What required teams of specialists, you can now do alone. What once cost millions in equipment and staff, you can now achieve from your laptop.

The Birth of the AI Polymath

In 2023, Marcus Chen was a mid-level marketing manager at a consumer products company in Seattle. His job was stable but specialized—he managed digital ad campaigns and occasionally contributed to content strategy. When his company announced layoffs, Marcus found himself competing against hundreds of other marketing specialists in a suddenly crowded job market.

Rather than doubling down on his specialty, Marcus took a different approach. Over six months, he immersed himself in AI tools across multiple domains:

- He learned Midjourney and DALL-E to create product visualization and marketing assets
- He used Claude and GPT-4 to draft marketing copy, business plans, and financial analyses
- He built simple web apps with no-code AI tools like Bubble and Zapier
- He created automated workflows that consolidated data from multiple sources

Today, Marcus runs a one-person agency that serves clients who previously required teams of 5-10 specialists. He handles everything from initial strategy to execution across branding, content creation, web development, analytics, and campaign management. His monthly income has tripled, and he works fewer hours than before.

Marcus isn't alone. From Toronto to Tokyo, Sydney to São Paulo, individuals are transforming themselves into one-person armies by mastering AI tools across disciplines.

The Four Powers of the AI Polymath

Becoming an AI polymath requires cultivating four fundamental powers that, when combined, create capabilities greater than the sum of their parts. These powers aren't just technical skills—they're transformation enablers that change what's possible for a single individual to accomplish.

1. The Power to Build

Software development once required years of training and specialized knowledge of programming languages. Today, the barrier to entry has collapsed. Tools like Replit Ghostwriter, GitHub Copilot, and Bolt allow anyone to create functional software by describing what they want in plain English.

Real-world example: Sarah Kim, a high school biology teacher with no coding background, used Bolt to create a custom learning app for her students. The app generates personalized quizzes based on each student's performance, visualizes concepts that students struggle with, and provides adaptive explanations. What would have previously required a development team and tens of thousands of dollars, Sarah created in a weekend at minimal cost.

The power to build extends beyond traditional software. With tools like Bubble, Webflow, and Framer, combined with AI assistance, you can create:

- Web applications with complex functionality
- Mobile apps deployable to app stores
- E-commerce platforms with custom features
- Automated data collection and analysis tools
- Interactive educational resources

The democratization of software creation means that the person who identifies a problem can immediately build a solution without intermediaries, delays, or dilution of their vision.

2. The Power to Automate

Naval Ravikant famously observed that wealth creation in the modern world comes down to leverage—ways to multiply your effort without multiplying the time you invest. Traditionally, there were three forms of leverage: labor (hiring people), capital (using money), and code/content (products with zero marginal cost of replication).

AI agents represent an entirely new form of leverage, combining elements of both labor and code. They're digital workers you can spawn instantly for a fraction of the cost of human labor, working 24/7 without complaint.

Real-world example: Miguel Ferreira, a solo consultant, built an AI-driven client acquisition system that:

- Monitors industry news and identifies potential clients experiencing challenges his services could address
- Generates personalized outreach messages referencing the specific challenge
- Manages follow-up communications on a schedule, with contextual awareness
- Prepares preliminary research dossiers on interested prospects
- Books meetings and sends reminders based on analyzing email responses

Miguel's system handles work that would previously have required a team of researchers, salespeople, and administrative staff. His close rate has increased by 35%, and he spends less than an hour daily on business development tasks that previously consumed most of his week.

The power to automate isn't just about creating individual agents. It extends to orchestrating entire workflows that connect multiple tools and processes into seamless systems. Using platforms like Zapier, Make.com, and n8n, combined with AI capabilities, you can create complex automation networks that:

- Move data between applications automatically
- Trigger actions based on specific conditions
- Process information according to business rules
- Generate reports and analytics
- Manage communication across channels

These automated systems become your digital workforce, handling routine tasks while you focus on high-value creative and strategic work.

3. The Power to Create

Professional-grade content creation once required expensive equipment, specialized training, and years of practice. Today, AI tools enable anyone to generate remarkable creative assets with minimal technical skill.

Real-world example: Alex Tomaro started a boutique travel agency focusing on custom Japanese travel experiences. Despite having no design background, Alex uses:

- Midjourney to create stunning visual assets for marketing materials
- Runway to generate promotional videos showcasing destinations
- Adobe Podcast and ElevenLabs to produce professional voiceovers in both English and Japanese
- Peachy for enhancing travel photos from customers into magazine-quality images
- Canva with AI capabilities to design polished presentations and itineraries

Alex's materials rival those produced by large agencies with dedicated creative departments. The professional aesthetic builds trust with high-end clients and has allowed his one-person operation to compete effectively against established firms.

The power to create extends across multiple formats and mediums:

- Visual: Generate and edit images, design marketing materials, create infographics
- Audio: Produce music, podcast intros, sound effects, and voice narration
- Video: Create animations, edit footage, generate b-roll and transitions
- Text: Write in multiple styles, from technical documentation to creative storytelling
- 3D: Build models, environments, and product visualizations

With each passing month, these tools improve in quality and ease of use. Already, the gap between AI-assisted amateurs and traditional professionals is narrowing—in some areas, it has disappeared entirely.

4. The Power to Connect

Building an audience and establishing influence once depended heavily on natural charisma, connections, or substantial marketing budgets. Today, AI tools enable anyone to build a following through consistent, high-quality content that resonates with specific audiences.

Real-world example: Jordan Harwick was a mechanical engineer with deep knowledge of sustainable energy systems but limited writing experience. Using AI tools to enhance his communication:

- He used Claude to help structure and refine complex technical concepts into accessible articles
- He created a content repurposing system that transformed each article into Twitter threads, LinkedIn posts, and newsletter segments
- He generated data visualizations that made energy concepts more understandable
- He used tools like Opus to create consistent visuals that strengthened his brand identity

Within 14 months, Jordan built a following of over 200,000 across platforms, landed a book deal, and launched a subscription newsletter generating $17,000 monthly. His success came not from outsourcing his thinking to AI but from using it to amplify his unique expertise and perspective.

The power to connect isn't just about building a large following—it's about forming meaningful relationships at scale. AI tools can help you:

- Identify the topics and formats that resonate most with your audience
- Maintain consistent engagement across multiple platforms
- Personalize communication to different segments
- Analyze feedback and adapt your approach
- Create systems for nurturing relationships over time

In an attention economy, the ability to build and maintain genuine connections represents an increasingly valuable form of capital.

Synergy: When Powers Combine

The true magic happens when these four powers amplify each other. Consider how each power enhances the others:

- **Build + Automate**: Create software tools that run themselves, handling tasks and making decisions without your intervention
- **Automate + Create**: Generate content at scale with systems that produce, refine, and distribute creative assets based on strategic inputs
- **Create + Connect**: Develop media that resonates deeply with specific audiences, building engagement that algorithms reward
- **Connect + Build**: Leverage audience feedback to develop tools and products perfectly aligned with market needs

A practical example of this synergy comes from independent creator Elena Martínez. Starting with zero audience, Elena:

1. **Built** a web application that analyzed trending topics in her industry
2. **Automated** a system to identify content gaps and generate preliminary outlines

3. **Created** Insightful articles and videos addressing those underserved topics
4. **Connected** with a growing audience by consistently delivering valuable content
5. Then, she **built** additional tools based on audience feedback, **automated** their distribution, **created** premium offerings, and **connected** with larger platforms and partners

Within 18 months, Elena had transformed from an unknown to an industry authority with a six-figure business—all without employees or outside investment.

The Polymath Advantage

AI polymaths enjoy several distinct advantages over both AI-resistant specialists and those who use AI narrowly within their existing specialties:

1. Adaptability

When market conditions change or technologies evolve, AI polymaths can quickly pivot. Their value isn't tied to a specific skill that might become obsolete but to their ability to leverage AI across domains.

2. Unique Combinations

The most valuable innovations often emerge at the intersection of disciplines. AI polymaths can make connections between fields that specialists miss, identifying opportunities that exist in the overlap.

3. Self-Sufficiency

By reducing or eliminating dependence on external specialists, AI polymaths can execute faster, maintain quality control, and capture more value from their work.

4. Reduced Overhead

Without the need to coordinate teams or manage complex workflows across departments, AI polymaths can operate with minimal administrative burden and lower costs.

5. Continuous Improvement

As AI capabilities expand, polymaths who have mastered the fundamental patterns of working with these tools can quickly adopt new advances, maintaining their competitive edge.

Becoming a Digital da Vinci: The Mindset Shift

The transition from specialist to AI polymath requires not just new skills but a fundamental shift in mindset. Traditional education and career paths have conditioned us to think in terms of credentials, specialization, and linear progression. Becoming an AI polymath means embracing:

Perpetual Learning

Accept that you'll never "arrive" at mastery. The tools and possibilities are evolving too quickly. Instead, focus on developing learning systems that help you rapidly absorb new capabilities.

Practical approach: Dedicate 30 minutes daily to exploring new AI tools. Create a personal knowledge base to document capabilities, prompts, and workflows that work for you.

Outcome Focus

Rather than identifying with specific tools or methods, define yourself by the outcomes you can achieve. This mental flexibility allows you to adopt new approaches without identity crisis.

Practical approach: When approaching a challenge, start by defining the desired end result, then work backward to identify the AI tools that could help you achieve it, regardless of whether they fall within your traditional skill set.

Intentional Generalization

While the world pushes for specialization, consciously resist narrowing your focus too much. Explore adjacent domains and seemingly unrelated fields for insights and capabilities you can incorporate.

Practical approach: For every deep dive you make into a specific tool or technique, allocate time to explore at least two complementary areas that could enhance your capability stack.

Bias Toward Action

The theoretical understanding of AI tools is far less valuable than practical experience using them. Prioritize hands-on experimentation over perfect knowledge.

Practical approach: Set challenges for yourself that require using multiple AI powers in combination. For example, create a weekend project to build a tool, automate its operation, create content about it, and share it with a relevant community.

Combinatorial Thinking

Train yourself to see connections between disparate tools and approaches. The most powerful workflows often involve unconventional combinations of AI capabilities.

Practical approach: Keep a "combinations journal" where you document interesting ways to connect different AI tools. Regularly review it for inspiration when tackling new projects.

The Journey Begins: Your First Steps

Becoming an AI polymath isn't achieved overnight, but you can begin the journey immediately. Here are concrete steps to take today:

1. **Assess your starting point**: Inventory your current capabilities across the four powers. Where are you strongest? Where do you need the most development?
2. **Choose your first power**: Based on your assessment and immediate needs, select one power to focus on initially. Master foundational tools in that area before expanding.
3. **Build your learning system**: Create a structured approach to discovering, testing, and incorporating new AI tools. This might include following key AI researchers on Twitter, joining communities of practice, or subscribing to newsletters that curate new developments.
4. **Start small, but start real**: Apply your developing capabilities to actual projects, not just tutorials or exercises. The complexity of real-world application forces deeper learning.
5. **Document everything**: Create your personal operating manual for working with AI tools. Record prompts that work well, combinations that yield interesting results, and workflows that save you time.

The Future Belongs to the Polymaths

As we move further into the AI era, the advantages of the polymath approach will become increasingly evident. Those who can harness AI to operate across domains will outcompete narrow specialists in most fields.

The one-person armies enabled by AI won't replace all larger organizations—complex projects and massive scale will still require coordination of multiple individuals. But the threshold of what a single person can accomplish will continue to rise dramatically.

In the words of Sam Altman, "The future belongs to those who can leverage AI to become many times more productive than they are today." By developing yourself into a Digital da Vinci—a modern polymath armed with AI capabilities across domains—you position yourself not just to survive but to thrive in the coming decades.

The tools at our disposal today would seem like magic to Leonardo da Vinci himself. What might you create with them?

Chapter 4: Code Without Coding: Building Software with Your Words, Not Your Keyboard

Throughout human history, our ability to create tools has defined our progress. From stone tools to steam engines to computers, each advancement has expanded what's possible for individuals to achieve. But until recently, one of the most powerful forms of creation—building software—remained locked behind a wall of technical knowledge.

For decades, creating even the simplest app required years of programming study. Those without coding skills were left with just two options: learn to code (a multi-year commitment) or hire developers (expensive and often frustrating). This limitation created a massive "creation gap" between what people could imagine and what they could actually build.

But in 2025, that gap is closing rapidly. AI-powered development tools are democratizing software creation in ways that would have seemed impossible just a few years ago. These tools allow you to build functional applications by describing what you want in plain English—without writing a single line of code yourself.

The End of the Coding Monopoly

Think about the last time you had an idea for a simple tool or app. Maybe it was a specialized calculator for your business, a custom booking system for your service, or just a unique way to organize information for yourself. In the pre-AI world, you faced a difficult choice:

1. Spend thousands of dollars hiring a developer
2. Invest hundreds of hours learning to code
3. Abandon your idea entirely

Most people chose option three, and countless potentially valuable tools were never created. The coding bottleneck meant that only a tiny percentage of software ideas ever saw the light of day.

AI-assisted development is changing this dynamic completely. As OpenAI's CTO Mira Murati put it, "We're entering an era where the limiting factor in software creation won't be technical skill, but imagination."

How AI-Assisted Development Works

At its core, AI-assisted development uses large language models to translate your natural language descriptions into functional code. You describe what you want—in plain English—and the AI generates the necessary code and assembles it into a working application.

The AI handles the technical complexity of:

- Choosing appropriate programming languages and frameworks
- Writing clean, efficient code
- Debugging and testing
- Integrating different components
- Building user interfaces

This process is similar to working with a human developer, but much faster and more affordable. You engage in a conversation with the AI, refining your requirements and seeing results in real-time.

Real-World AI Development Tools

Let's explore some of the leading AI-assisted development tools available in 2025 and what they're capable of:

1. GitHub Copilot Studio
GitHub Copilot has evolved from a simple code completion tool into a full-fledged development environment. Copilot Studio allows you to:

- Generate entire applications from natural language descriptions
- Create functional user interfaces by describing their components
- Build and deploy web applications without touching code
- Integrate with databases and APIs through simple instructions

Example Use Case: A person using Copilot Studio can create a custom retirement calculator by describing the inputs needed (current age, savings, expected retirement age), the calculation logic, and how they want the results displayed. Within an hour, they could have a professional-looking web app to share with clients.

2. Replit Ghost

Replit's AI agent, called Ghost, takes AI-assisted coding to a new level by functioning as a pair programmer that can:

- Create entire applications from scratch based on your descriptions
- Modify existing code based on your feedback
- Explain how the code works in simple terms
- Deploy applications to the web with a single command

Example Use Case: A person using Replit Ghost could build an interactive quiz platform for students by simply describing what they want—multiple-choice questions, instant feedback, and a leaderboard. Ghost would generate the app, and adding features like timed quizzes would be as easy as telling it what's needed.

3. Vercel's Next.js AI

Vercel has integrated AI deeply into their Next.js framework, creating a system that can:

- Generate full-stack web applications from text prompts
- Create responsive, accessible user interfaces
- Connect to various data sources and APIs
- Implement complex business logic without you writing code

Example Use Case: A person using Next.js AI could create an online ordering system for a small bakery by describing the menu items, pricing, delivery options, and payment preferences. The AI would generate a complete ordering system with a beautiful interface and allow them to add additional features, like a loyalty program, by simply describing it.

4. Bubble AI
Bubble has been a leader in no-code development for years, but their AI capabilities have transformed the platform into something far more powerful:

- Visual interface combined with AI assistance
- Natural language to create complex workflows
- AI-generated plugins and integrations
- Automatic database schema creation based on descriptions

Example Use Case: A person using Bubble AI can create a client portal for their freelance photography business. By describing the workflow— image uploading, client feedback, and user authentication—the AI would generate the entire application and system without the need for coding.

5. Microsoft Power Apps Copilot
Microsoft has integrated AI deeply into their Power Platform, allowing business users to:

- Create business applications through conversation
- Automatically generate database structures
- Build mobile apps from spreadsheets or descriptions
- Implement complex business logic without coding

Example Use Case: A person using Power Apps Copilot can quickly build an employee onboarding application by describing the process, required documents, and workflows. The AI would generate the application, integrating it with their company's existing Microsoft systems, and make it easy to update as regulations change.

6. WIzed AI

Wized combines visual building with AI assistance to let you:

- Create web applications through conversation
- Design custom interfaces that adapt to your branding
- Implement complex data handling without SQL knowledge
- Connect to third-party services with natural language

Example Use Case: A person using Wized AI can create a membership management system for a small gym. By describing membership tiers, scheduling needs, and payment requirements, the AI would generate a complete system, including features like class booking and fitness progress tracking.

7. Framer AI

Framer has evolved from a design tool to a complete development platform that can:

- Generate interactive websites from text descriptions
- Create animations and transitions through natural language
- Build interactive prototypes that feel like real applications
- Deploy production-ready websites with no coding

Example Use Case: A person using Framer AI can build a product launch website by describing the product features, pricing, and desired storytelling approach. The AI would generate the entire website, complete with animations, interactive elements, and responsive design.

8. Durable AI

Durable focuses on helping entrepreneurs build complete business websites and apps:

- Generate entire business websites from a description
- Create online booking systems without coding

- Build customer management systems through conversation
- Implement payment processing with simple instructions

Example Use Case: A person using Durable AI could build a business website for a home cleaning service by describing the services offered, pricing, and availability. The AI would generate a complete website with integrated booking and payment processing, making it easy to manage appointments and process payments.

The Building Process: A Step-by-Step Example

To understand how these tools work in practice, let's walk through the process of building a simple application using AI-assisted development:

1. **Idea Clarification**: You start by clearly defining what you want to build. For example, "I want to create a meal planning app that generates weekly meal plans based on dietary preferences, generates shopping lists, and allows users to save favorite recipes."
2. **Initial Generation**: You enter this description into your AI development tool (let's say Replit Ghost), and it generates a basic version of the application with core functionality.
3. **Iterative Refinement**: You review what the AI created and provide feedback: "The meal planning part looks good, but can you add filters for allergies and make the shopping list exportable to PDF?"
4. **Feature Addition**: The AI implements your requested changes, generating the necessary code behind the scenes.
5. **Testing and Feedback**: You test the application, noting any issues or desired improvements: "The allergy filters work well, but I'd like to add a calorie calculator for each meal."
6. **Finalization**: After a few rounds of feedback, the AI finalizes the application according to your specifications.
7. **Deployment**: The tool helps you deploy your application to make it available to users.

What would have taken weeks or months of development work is compressed into hours or days, with no coding required from you.

Limitations and Best Practices

While these AI development tools are revolutionary, they do have limitations:

Current Limitations

1. **Complexity Ceiling**: These tools excel at straightforward applications but may struggle with highly complex systems or cutting-edge functionality.
2. **Integration Challenges**: Connecting to specialized third-party services sometimes requires technical knowledge.
3. **Customization Depth**: Highly specific or unusual features may require some manual coding adjustments.
4. **Performance Optimization**: AI-generated applications may not be as optimized as those built by experienced developers.

Best Practices for Success

1. **Start Simple**: Begin with a clear, focused application idea rather than trying to build something massive right away.
2. **Use Iterative Development**: Build the core functionality first, then add features incrementally.
3. **Provide Clear Descriptions**: The more clearly you can describe what you want, the better results you'll get.
4. **Learn Basic Concepts**: Understanding fundamental concepts like databases, APIs, and user interfaces will help you communicate with AI tools more effectively.
5. **Combine Tools When Needed**: Sometimes using multiple AI tools for different aspects of your project yields better results.

How to Start Building Today

Ready to start creating your own applications without coding? Here's a simple path to get started:

1. **Identify Your First Project**: Choose something simple but useful— a personal tool, a business process automator, or a simple website with specific functionality.

2. **Select the Right Tool**: Based on your project type, choose one of the AI development platforms mentioned earlier. Many offer free tiers to experiment with.
3. **Learn Through Building**: The best way to learn is by doing. Start creating and learn as you go, using the AI's guidance.
4. **Join Communities**: Platforms like Replit, Bubble, and GitHub have active communities where you can learn from others and share your projects.
5. **Iterate and Improve**: Your first version won't be perfect, and that's okay. Gather feedback and use it to improve your application over time.

The Future: Building Beyond Current Limitations

As powerful as today's AI development tools are, they're improving rapidly. What can we expect in the near future?

- **Increased Complexity Handling**: AI will soon manage enterprise-grade applications with complex business logic.
- **Better Performance Optimization**: AI will generate code that's increasingly efficient and scalable.
- **Domain-Specific Expertise**: AI tools will develop specialized knowledge in areas like healthcare, finance, and education.
- **Collaborative Intelligence**: AI will work alongside human developers more seamlessly, handling routine tasks while humans focus on innovation.

Conclusion: Your New Superpower

The ability to create software without coding is not just a convenience—it's a superpower. It removes one of the biggest barriers to innovation and puts the power of creation in everyone's hands.

In a world where so many jobs and skills are becoming automated, the ability to envision and create new tools becomes increasingly valuable. AI-assisted development doesn't replace the need for human creativity—it amplifies it.

As we move further into the AI age, the question is no longer "Can I build it?" but "What should I build?" The technical barriers are falling, leaving only the limits of your imagination.

The software development monopoly has ended. The era of universal creation has begun.

Chapter 5: Your Digital Workforce: Creating AI Agents That Work While You Sleep

In the evolving landscape of AI, perhaps nothing is more transformative than the ability to create your own digital workforce—autonomous AI agents that handle tasks while you focus elsewhere or even sleep. As Naval Ravikant observed, success in the modern world comes down to leverage—ways to multiply your effort without multiplying your time. AI agents represent an entirely new form of leverage, combining the scalability of code with the capabilities of human labor.

The Dawn of Personal AI Workforces

Imagine waking up to discover your digital employees have:

- Responded to all your customer emails
- Scheduled your meetings for the week
- Generated social media content
- Analyzed your business data
- Summarized important news in your industry
- Added qualified leads to your sales pipeline

This isn't science fiction—it's happening now. AI agents can work 24/7 without breaks, complaints, or salary negotiations. They scale instantly and cost a fraction of human labor. Most importantly, they're becoming accessible to everyone, not just tech experts or large corporations.

What Are AI Agents Exactly?

At their core, AI agents are autonomous systems designed to perform specific tasks with minimal human supervision. Unlike basic automation which follows rigid rules, AI agents can:

- Make decisions based on changing circumstances
- Learn from past performance
- Handle ambiguity and exceptions
- Coordinate with other tools and systems
- Process and respond to natural language

The best agents combine the problem-solving capabilities of large language models with the ability to use tools, access data, and execute actions in the digital world.

The Building Blocks of Your Digital Workforce

Creating effective AI agents requires understanding three key components:

1. The Brain: Foundation Models

Every agent needs intelligence. This comes from large language models (LLMs) like:

- **OpenAI's GPT-4o**: The most powerful commercial LLM for general-purpose agents
- **Claude 3.5 Sonnet**: Excels at complex reasoning and following nuanced instructions
- **Anthropic's Claude Opus**: Strong at tasks requiring careful analysis and judgment
- **Mistral Large**: An excellent open-source alternative for cost-effective deployment
- **Google's Gemini Pro**: Particularly strong for agents that need multimodal capabilities

Think of these as the "brains" that power your agents. Different models excel at different tasks, and the best agent setups often use multiple models based on the specific needs.

2. The Body: Tools and Integrations

Intelligence without the ability to take action is limited. AI agents need tools to interact with the digital world:

- **API Access**: Connecting to services like Google Calendar, Gmail, or Slack
- **Browser Control**: Navigating websites and filling forms

- **Database Operations**: Reading and writing to your business systems
- **File System Access**: Managing documents and processing information
- **Communication Tools**: Sending emails, messages, or notifications

The more tools your agent can access, the more versatile and valuable it becomes.

3. The Memory: Knowledge and Context

Effective agents need access to:

- **Your Data**: Documents, emails, calendars, CRM information
- **Procedural Knowledge**: How your business processes work
- **Historical Context**: Past interactions and decisions
- **Real-time Information**: Current status of projects and systems

With these three components—intelligence, tools, and memory—you can build agents that handle increasingly complex workflows.

Building Your First Agents: No-Code Solutions

The easiest way to start creating AI agents is through no-code platforms that handle the technical complexity:

AutoGPT

AutoGPT allows you to create autonomous agents with specific goals. You provide a mission statement, and the agent breaks it down into steps, executes them, and adapts as needed.

Example Use Case: Research competitors in your industry. Tell AutoGPT to analyze 10 competitors, gather pricing information, identify unique features, and create a comparison table—all while you're asleep.

Relevance AI

Relevance AI offers a visual interface for building complex agents without coding. It excels at connecting multiple data sources and tools.

Example Use Case: Create a lead qualification agent that monitors your website forms, researches new leads on LinkedIn, scores them based on your criteria, and routes high-quality prospects directly to your sales team.

OpenAI Assistants

OpenAI Assistants provides a straightforward way to create specialized agents with access to custom knowledge and tools.

Example Use Case: Build a customer support agent that answers product questions, references your knowledge base, troubleshoots common issues, and creates support tickets when it can't solve a problem.

AgentGPT

AgentGPT focuses on simplicity and accessibility, letting you create and deploy agents through a user-friendly interface.

Example Use Case: Deploy a content repurposing agent that takes your blog posts, creates social media versions for different platforms, schedules them for optimal times, and tracks engagement.

LangChain

For those with minimal coding experience, **LangChain** provides templates and pre-built components for agent creation.

Example Use Case: Develop an email management agent that categorizes incoming messages, drafts responses to common inquiries, flags important communications, and follows up on unanswered emails.

Advanced Agent Orchestration

As your digital workforce grows, you'll need systems to coordinate multiple agents:

Zapier

Zapier connects over 5,000 apps and can serve as the central nervous system for your agent ecosystem.

Example Use Case: When a new lead comes in through your website, Zapier triggers your research agent to gather information, your qualification agent to score the lead, and your outreach agent to send a personalized message—all working in sequence.

Make.com (formerly Integromat)

Make.com offers more advanced workflow capabilities for complex agent orchestration.

Example Use Case: Create a social media content pipeline where one agent generates ideas, another creates drafts, a third produces images, and a fourth handles publishing and community management.

n8n

For those needing maximum flexibility, **n8n** provides an open-source workflow automation platform.

Example Use Case: Build a comprehensive customer onboarding system where different agents handle welcome emails, account setup, initial training, feedback collection, and early warning systems for potential churn.

Real-World Agent Workflows That Make Money While You Sleep

Let's explore specific agent systems that deliver real business value:

Lead Generation and Qualification System

Components:

- **Prospecting Agent**: Uses Apollo.io and LinkedIn Sales Navigator to identify potential customers
- **Research Agent**: Gathers company information, recent news, and potential pain points
- **Personalization Agent**: Crafts custom outreach messages based on research
- **Follow-up Agent**: Manages the cadence of communications until response

Tools:

- OpenAI's GPT-4 for intelligence
- Relevance AI for orchestration
- LinkedIn Sales Navigator API
- Apollo.io for contact information
- Gmail API for communication

This system can generate 50-100 qualified leads per day with thoughtful, personalized outreach that doesn't feel automated.

Content Creation and Distribution Engine

Components:

- **Topic Research Agent**: Identifies trending subjects and keyword opportunities
- **Content Creation Agent**: Drafts articles, scripts, or social posts
- **Media Generation Agent**: Creates supporting images or video clips
- **Publishing Agent**: Formats and posts content to appropriate platforms
- **Engagement Agent**: Monitors and responds to comments

Tools:

- Claude 3 Opus for nuanced writing
- DALL·E 3 for image generation
- Zapier for workflow management
- WordPress, Medium, and social media APIs

- Buffer for scheduling

This system can maintain a consistent content schedule across multiple channels without daily intervention.

Customer Support Optimization

Components:

- **Triage Agent**: Categorizes incoming support requests by urgency and type
- **Resolution Agent**: Handles common questions and problems
- **Escalation Agent**: Creates detailed tickets for complex issues
- **Follow-up Agent**: Checks on customer satisfaction after resolution

Tools:

- GPT-4o for understanding customer needs
- Zendesk or Intercom integration
- Knowledge base access via embeddings
- CRM integration for customer history

This system can handle 80% of routine support queries automatically, drastically reducing response times and support costs.

E-commerce Optimization Suite

Components:

- **Inventory Management Agent**: Monitors stock levels and suggests reorders
- **Pricing Agent**: Adjusts prices based on competitor analysis and demand
- **Product Description Agent**: Creates and updates product listings
- **Customer Behavior Agent**: Analyzes shopping patterns and suggests promotions
- **Abandoned Cart Agent**: Sends personalized recovery emails

Tools:

- Shopify or WooCommerce API
- Competitor price monitoring tools
- Customer data analytics
- Email marketing platform integration

This system can increase conversion rates by 15-30% through timely interventions and optimizations.

Beyond Basic Agents: Creating Learning Systems

The most powerful agent systems improve over time. Here's how to build this capability:

Feedback Loops

Design your agents to collect data on their performance:

- Which emails get responses?
- Which content generates engagement?
- When do humans need to intervene?

Use this information to continuously refine your agents.

A/B Testing

Create multiple versions of your agents with different approaches:

- Different communication styles
- Various decision thresholds
- Alternative workflow sequences

Let data determine which approaches work best.

Human-in-the-Loop Refinement

The most effective agent systems maintain a role for human oversight:

- Review agent decisions above certain thresholds
- Provide feedback on agent outputs
- Periodically audit agent performance
- Update agent instructions based on changing business needs

Common Pitfalls and How to Avoid Them

As you build your digital workforce, watch out for these common issues:

Scope Creep

Problem: Creating agents that try to do too much leads to poor performance. **Solution**: Start with narrowly defined agents focused on specific tasks.

Insufficient Monitoring

Problem: Agents running without oversight can drift off-course. **Solution**: Implement logging, alerts for unusual patterns, and regular performance reviews.

Privacy and Security Risks

Problem: Agents with broad access can create security vulnerabilities. **Solution**: Follow the principle of least privilege—give agents only the access they absolutely need.

Overreliance

Problem: Becoming too dependent on agents without understanding their limitations. **Solution**: Maintain human checkpoints for critical decisions and operations.

Starting Your Agent Journey: A 30-Day Plan

Here's how to build your first effective agent system in just one month:

Days 1-7: Analysis and Planning

- Audit your current workflows
- Identify repetitive, time-consuming tasks
- Prioritize processes with clear inputs and outputs
- Document your standard operating procedures

Days 8-14: First Agent Creation

- Select a no-code platform like Relevance AI or OpenAI Assistants
- Build a single-purpose agent for your highest-priority task
- Test extensively with varied inputs
- Refine prompts and instructions

Days 15-21: Integration and Tools

- Connect your agent to necessary data sources
- Add tool capabilities (email, calendar, CRM)
- Create monitoring and logging systems
- Develop error handling procedures

Days 22-30: Expansion and Orchestration

- Add 2-3 complementary agents
- Build workflows connecting their operations
- Implement feedback collection
- Create a dashboard for oversight

By the end of 30 days, you'll have a functioning agent system handling real work while you focus on higher-value activities.

The Near Future: What's Coming in Agent Technology

The field is evolving rapidly. Here's what to watch for:

Agentic Operating Systems

Platforms like Fixie.ai and E2B are creating specialized environments designed specifically for running multiple AI agents that can collaborate more effectively.

Multi-Agent Collaboration

Beyond simple workflows, research is advancing on systems where agents can work together, specializing in different aspects of complex tasks.

Enhanced Memory and Learning

Agents will soon maintain more sophisticated long-term memory and improve their performance based on accumulated experience.

Vision-Enabled Agents

Advances in multimodal AI are creating agents that can process and understand visual information, dramatically expanding their capabilities.

The Bottom Line: Competitive Advantage

As we move toward 2025 and beyond, having a skilled digital workforce will be a fundamental competitive advantage. Those who master agent creation will:

- Complete more work with fewer resources
- Respond faster to market changes
- Operate efficiently at all hours
- Scale operations without proportional cost increases
- Focus human talent on truly creative and strategic work

The greatest leverage in business has always gone to those who can accomplish more with less. AI agents represent the next evolution of this principle—enabling individuals and small teams to achieve what once required entire departments.

By starting now with even simple agents, you'll develop the skills and understanding needed to thrive as this technology matures. Your digital workforce doesn't replace you—it amplifies you, working tirelessly behind the scenes to turn your vision into reality, even while you sleep.

Chapter 6: The Creative Alchemist: Turning Prompts into Professional-Grade Content

In the emerging AI economy, the ability to generate professional-grade creative content quickly and affordably represents a fundamental competitive advantage. What once required specialized training, expensive equipment, and years of experience can now be accomplished through well-crafted prompts and the right AI tools. This chapter explores how anyone can become a "creative alchemist" – transforming simple text instructions into valuable creative assets across multiple mediums.

The Democratization of Creativity

For most of human history, creative production has been limited by technical skill barriers. A business needing visual assets would hire a designer. A website requiring copy would engage a writer. A marketing campaign requiring video would contract a production company. Each creative discipline demanded years of specialized training and often expensive tools.

The AI revolution has fundamentally altered this paradigm. Today, a single person with no formal creative training can generate images, write copy, edit videos, compose music, and design interfaces – all through the strategic use of AI tools guided by thoughtful prompts.

As Kevin Kelly noted, "The printing press democratized knowledge, the camera democratized images, and AI is democratizing creativity itself." We are witnessing the birth of a new creative class – not defined by technical mastery of specific tools, but by conceptual thinking and prompt engineering skills.

The AI Creative Suite: Tools of the Trade

Let's examine the specific AI tools transforming various creative disciplines and how you can leverage them to produce professional-grade content.

Visual Content Creation

Image Generation Tools

- **Midjourney**: Currently producing some of the most aesthetically pleasing AI-generated images, Midjourney excels at artistic renderings, conceptual illustrations, and realistic visualizations. Through Discord integration, users can generate images by typing "/imagine" followed by detailed descriptions.
- **DALL-E**: OpenAI's image generation model excels at following specific instructions and generating images that match precise requirements. Its web interface allows for quick iterations and edits to existing images.
- **Stable Diffusion**: An open-source alternative that can be run locally or accessed through various interfaces like DreamStudio. Particularly useful for creating variations of existing images or incorporating specific visual elements.
- **Leonardo.AI**: Specializes in game assets, character design, and consistent visual styles across multiple images. Also offers the ability to train custom models on specific visual styles.

Effective Image Prompting Techniques:

1. **Be specific about style**: "Create a minimalist logo with geometric shapes in blue and teal, inspired by Scandinavian design" rather than "Make a modern logo."
2. **Reference specific artists or movements**: "Generate a landscape in the style of Hudson River School painters" rather than "Make a pretty landscape."
3. **Specify technical parameters**: "Create a top-down isometric view of a modern office space with soft natural lighting" rather than "Show me an office."
4. **Use aspect ratio commands**: "Create a 16:9 wide cinematic shot of a futuristic city skyline at sunset" to get dimensions suitable for specific use cases.
5. **Iterate and refine**: Save promising generations and use them as the basis for further refinement with commands like "Make the colors more vibrant" or "Add more detail to the foreground."

Video Content Creation

AI Video Tools

- **Runway Gen-2**: Creates short video clips from text prompts or extends existing footage with AI-generated content. Particularly useful for creating atmospheric b-roll, transitions, and abstract visualizations.
- **Pika Labs**: Specializes in character animations and transformations, allowing users to generate dynamic scenes from static images or text descriptions.
- **Synthesia**: Creates talking-head videos with AI avatars that can deliver scripts in multiple languages. Useful for training videos, presentations, and simple explainer content.
- **HeyGen**: Produces AI spokesperson videos with customizable avatars and voices. Allows for script editing and facial expressions that match the content.
- **Descript**: While primarily a video editor, its AI features like automatic transcription, filler word removal, and the ability to edit video by editing text make it extremely powerful for post-production.

Effective Video Prompting Techniques:

1. **Describe motion explicitly**: "A slow camera pan across a desk with office supplies, moving from left to right" rather than "Show me a desk."
2. **Specify camera angles and movements**: "A bird's-eye view slowly zooming in on a busy intersection" rather than "Show me a city."
3. **Break complex videos into scenes**: Generate individual scenes and then combine them rather than trying to create complex narratives in a single prompt.
4. **Consider mood and lighting**: "A tense scene with dramatic shadows and low-key lighting" helps set the emotional tone.
5. **Reference familiar visual styles**: "Create a product showcase in the style of Apple commercials with clean backgrounds and dramatic lighting" leverages established visual languages.

Audio and Music Creation

AI Audio Tools

- **Suno**: Creates original music tracks in various genres from text descriptions. Can generate complete songs with lyrics and vocals that match specific themes or emotions.
- **AIVA**: Specializes in compositional music for different moods and applications, particularly useful for background tracks and instrumental pieces.
- **ElevenLabs**: Produces ultra-realistic voice narration that can match tone, accent, and emotional inflection. Useful for voiceovers, audiobooks, and podcast content.
- **Soundraw**: Generates royalty-free music tracks that can be customized by mood, tempo, instruments, and length. Particularly useful for creating background music for videos.
- **AudioPen**: Cleans up audio recordings, removing background noise and enhancing voice quality. Can also generate environmental sound effects from text descriptions.

Effective Audio Prompting Techniques:

1. **Specify genre and influences**: "Create an upbeat jazz track influenced by 1950s bebop with prominent saxophone" rather than "Make happy music."
2. **Describe emotional trajectory**: "Compose a piece that begins contemplatively, builds tension in the middle, and resolves triumphantly" to guide the emotional arc.
3. **Reference specific instruments and techniques**: "Create a lo-fi hip hop beat with vinyl crackle, sidechained kick drum, and muted jazz piano samples" for technical specificity.
4. **For voice generation, include direction on delivery**: "Narrate this text in a warm, conversational tone with slight pauses for emphasis at key points" rather than simply providing the text.
5. **When generating sound effects, describe physical properties**: "Create the sound of heavy rainfall on a metal roof with occasional thunder in the distance" provides contextual information.

Written Content Creation

AI Writing Tools

- **Claude**: Excels at longer-form creative writing, maintaining coherent narrative and consistent tone across thousands of words. Particularly strong for storytelling, article writing, and marketing copy.
- **ChatGPT**: Versatile for various writing tasks including drafting emails, creating social media copy, and generating business documents. Its memory within a conversation allows for iterative refinement.
- **Jasper**: Purpose-built for marketing content with templates for specific formats like Facebook ads, product descriptions, and blog posts. Includes tools for maintaining brand voice.
- **PerplexityAI**: Combines language model capabilities with web search for fact-checking and current information. Useful for research-based writing and fact-centered content.
- **Writesonic**: Specializes in SEO-optimized content with tools for generating meta descriptions, keyword optimization, and content structured for search visibility.

Effective Writing Prompting Techniques:

1. **Specify audience and purpose**: "Write a technical explanation of blockchain for finance professionals who are considering implementing the technology" rather than "Explain blockchain."
2. **Include format guidance**: "Create a 500-word blog post with 3-4 subheadings, short paragraphs, and a conversational tone" to shape the structural elements.
3. **Provide examples of desired style**: "Write in the clear, direct style of Hemingway, with short sentences and minimal adjectives" gives a clear stylistic reference.
4. **For marketing copy, specify the emotional response**: "Write product description copy that creates a sense of exclusivity and urgency for luxury watch buyers" targets specific psychological triggers.

5. **Use system prompts for consistent voice**: "You are writing as the voice of a friendly, knowledgeable science teacher who uses analogies to explain complex topics" establishes a consistent persona.

Combining AI Creative Tools for Compound Effects

The true power of these creative AI tools emerges when they're used in combination. Consider these workflows that leverage multiple AI tools for comprehensive content creation:

Case Study: Creating a Product Launch Campaign

1. **Start with strategy**: Use Claude to outline a marketing strategy and key messaging points for the product launch.
2. **Generate visual assets**: Use Midjourney to create product imagery, lifestyle photos, and promotional graphics based on the messaging.
3. **Develop video content**: Use Runway to create short promotional clips and product demonstrations.
4. **Create audio elements**: Use Suno to compose a signature sound for the brand and ElevenLabs for voiceover narration.
5. **Produce written content**: Use PerplexityAI to research market conditions and Claude to write press releases, social media copy, and website content.
6. **Edit and refine**: Use Descript to edit video content and combine all elements into a cohesive campaign.

This integrated approach allows a single person to produce what would traditionally require an entire creative agency and production company.

Case Study: Developing Educational Content

1. **Research and outline**: Use PerplexityAI to gather accurate information on the subject matter and Claude to develop a comprehensive course outline.
2. **Create visual explanations**: Use DALL-E to generate diagrams, charts, and visual aids that illustrate key concepts.

3. **Develop video lectures**: Use Synthesia to create talking-head videos explaining complex topics.
4. **Create supporting materials**: Use Claude to write accompanying notes, quizzes, and exercises.
5. **Design interactive elements**: Use AI-assisted development tools to create simple interactive demonstrations or quizzes.

This workflow enables a subject matter expert to develop professional educational content without needing design or video production skills.

Common Challenges and Solutions

While AI creative tools offer unprecedented capabilities, they come with challenges that must be addressed to produce truly professional results:

Challenge: Inconsistency Across Generated Assets

Solution: Create detailed style guides for your AI prompts. Maintain consistent descriptors for style, mood, color palette, and composition across all generations. Save successful outputs and use them as reference points for future generations with commands like "Use this same style for..."

Challenge: Limited Control Over Specific Details

Solution: Break complex creative tasks into smaller components that you generate separately and then combine. For example, rather than trying to generate a complete website design in one prompt, create individual UI elements and arrange them yourself.

Challenge: Output Quality Plateaus

Solution: Learn to use model-specific advanced techniques. For instance, with Midjourney, understanding parameters like --stylize, --chaos, and --quality dramatically improves results. With language models, learning prompt engineering techniques like chain-of-thought and few-shot prompting elevates output quality.

Challenge: Copyright and Originality Concerns

Solution: Use AI outputs as starting points rather than final products. Incorporate your own modifications, combinations, and refinements to ensure originality. Be aware of the training data limitations of different models, and avoid explicitly requesting copyrighted styles or characters.

Challenge: AI "Hallmarks" and Telltale Signs

Solution: Develop an eye for AI-specific artifacts like unusual hands in Midjourney images or repetitive phrasing in AI writing. Learn post-processing techniques to address these issues, such as targeted image editing or manual rewriting of problematic passages.

Beyond Technical Tools: The Mindset of the Creative Alchemist

The most successful AI creative practitioners develop specific mental approaches that maximize these tools:

1. **Conceptual Thinking**: Focus on developing unique concepts and creative direction rather than technical execution. The idea becomes more important than the implementation.
2. **Iterative Refinement**: Embrace rapid prototyping and iteration. Generate multiple variations quickly, identify the strongest elements, and refine rather than expecting perfection initially.
3. **Cross-Disciplinary Vision**: Think across creative disciplines. Consider how visual, written, and audio elements can complement each other rather than working in isolated creative silos.
4. **Curation Skills**: Develop a sharp eye for selecting the best outputs from multiple generations. The ability to recognize quality becomes as important as the ability to create it.
5. **System Design**: Think in terms of repeatable creative systems rather than one-off projects. Design prompt templates and workflows that can be applied across multiple contexts.

The Ethical Creative

As you develop your AI creative capabilities, consider these ethical principles:

1. **Transparency**: Be open about AI usage when appropriate, particularly in professional contexts where disclosure expectations exist.
2. **Attribution**: Acknowledge the human creators whose work trained the AI models you're using, particularly when drawing inspiration from specific artists or styles.
3. **Originality**: Use AI as a collaborative tool rather than a replacement for human creativity. The most compelling AI-assisted work combines algorithmic capabilities with human direction and refinement.
4. **Environmental Awareness**: Recognize that AI model training and inference have environmental impacts. Use these tools thoughtfully rather than generating excessive outputs unnecessarily.
5. **Inclusive Design**: Be mindful of biases in AI systems, particularly around representation of different cultures and identities. Take steps to ensure your creative outputs are inclusive and respectful.

Looking Ahead: The Future of AI Creativity

The tools discussed in this chapter represent just the beginning of AI's creative capabilities. Looking ahead, we can anticipate:

1. **Greater Control**: Future generations of creative AI will offer more precise control over specific elements and details.
2. **Multimodal Integration**: Tools will seamlessly blend text, image, video, and audio generation in unified creative environments.
3. **Personalized Creative Models**: The ability to fine-tune models on personal or brand-specific styles will become more accessible and effective.
4. **Collaborative Interfaces**: AI creative tools will evolve to better support human-AI collaboration with more intuitive interfaces and feedback mechanisms.

5. **Democratized Professional Tools**: Enterprise-grade creative capabilities will become increasingly accessible to individuals and small businesses.

Conclusion: The New Creative Economy

The ability to transform prompts into professional-grade creative content represents more than just a technical skill—it's a fundamental shift in how creative value is produced and exchanged in our economy.

As these tools continue to evolve, the gap between idea and execution narrows dramatically. The limiting factor becomes not technical skill or production resources, but the quality of your conceptual thinking and your ability to direct these powerful AI systems.

In this new creative landscape, success belongs not to those with the most specialized technical training, but to those who can envision unique possibilities and articulate them effectively to their AI collaborators. The creative alchemist—turning simple prompts into valuable assets—represents the new model of creative professional in the AI age.

Chapter 7: Influence Amplified: Building Your Audience and Brand in the AI Era

The New Currency: Attention and Trust

In today's digital landscape, attention has become the most valuable commodity. As traditional career paths become increasingly disrupted by AI, your ability to build and maintain an audience isn't just a nice-to-have—it's essential for professional survival.

Consider this: When employers, clients, or customers search for you online, what do they find? Is it a compelling digital presence that showcases your expertise, or is it silence? In the AI era, being invisible online is the equivalent of not existing professionally.

The greatest value of building an audience isn't just the immediate opportunities it creates, but the compound interest that accrues over time. Each piece of content you publish, each meaningful interaction you have online, adds to your digital reputation—a currency that appreciates rather than depreciates.

Why Building an Audience Matters Now More Than Ever

The rise of AI has fundamentally changed the game for personal branding in three critical ways:

1. **Barrier to entry has crashed**: Creating professional-quality content used to require specialized skills, expensive equipment, and years of practice. Today, AI tools enable anyone to produce compelling content—making it both easier to start and more necessary to stand out.
2. **Career insurance in uncertain times**: As traditional jobs face disruption, your audience becomes your safety net. It represents a network of opportunities that exists independently of any single employer or platform.
3. **Exponential value creation**: Every piece of content you create has the potential to work for you 24/7, reaching people while you sleep and opening doors you didn't even know existed.

The Four Pillars of AI-Enhanced Audience Building

Building an audience in the AI era rests on four fundamental pillars, each of which can be dramatically enhanced with the right AI tools:

1. Content Creation: From Blank Page to Brilliant Ideas

The most common obstacle to building an audience is the dreaded blank page. Even experts who know their subject matter intimately often struggle to transform their knowledge into engaging content.

AI writing assistants have revolutionized this process by serving as thought partners rather than replacements. They help you explore ideas, overcome writer's block, and refine your thinking.

Key AI Tools for Content Creation:

- **Claude by Anthropic**: Excels at helping you explore ideas in depth and craft nuanced content that reflects your authentic voice. Particularly useful for longer-form content where complex ideas need careful explanation.
- **ChatGPT**: Useful for quick brainstorming sessions and generating multiple angles on a topic. The "continue writing" feature helps maintain flow when you're stuck.
- **Jasper**: Specifically designed for marketing content, with templates for blog posts, social media, and email campaigns. Its "tone of voice" feature helps maintain consistency across platforms.
- **Writesonic**: Specializes in SEO-optimized content with its "Article Writer 5.0" feature that analyzes top-ranking content to inform your writing strategy.
- **HypotenusAI**: Uses your notes, research, and specific instructions to generate first drafts of articles that sound like you wrote them.

Practical Application Strategy:

Instead of asking AI to "write a blog post about personal branding," try this workflow:

1. Use AI to explore your specific angle: "Help me brainstorm 10 unique perspectives on personal branding for software developers transitioning to AI roles."
2. Select the most compelling angle and ask: "Let's outline a comprehensive article on how software developers can showcase their AI adaptation skills through strategic personal branding."
3. For each section, use AI to explore ideas deeper: "For the section on 'Demonstrating Technical Adaptability,' help me develop three concrete examples with actionable details."
4. After drafting, use AI for refinement: "Review this section for clarity and suggest ways to make the advice more actionable and specific."

This approach ensures you remain the architect of your ideas while leveraging AI as a powerful thought partner.

2. Content Strategy: Building a Coherent Narrative

Random content, no matter how well-crafted, won't build a loyal audience. You need a coherent strategy that positions you as an authority in your field and delivers consistent value.

Key AI Tools for Content Strategy:

- **BuzzSumo**: Uses AI to analyze millions of articles and social posts to identify trending topics and content formats in your niche.
- **MarketMuse**: Applies AI to identify content gaps in your industry that you can fill, along with difficulty scores to prioritize your efforts.
- **Clearscope**: Analyzes top-performing content for any topic and provides AI-driven recommendations to optimize your content for both search engines and human readers.
- **Lately**: Uses AI to analyze your best-performing content and create a content strategy based on what resonates with your audience.
- **Cohesive**: Creates AI-driven content calendars by analyzing your audience data, industry trends, and performance metrics.

Practical Application Strategy:

1. Use BuzzSumo to identify trending topics in your niche.
2. Input those topics into MarketMuse to find specific angles that aren't yet saturated.
3. Create a content calendar that balances timely topics with evergreen content.
4. Use Claude or ChatGPT to develop a consistent framework for your content (like a signature structure for articles or videos).

3. Content Distribution: Reaching the Right People

Creating great content is only half the battle. To build an audience, you need to get your content in front of the right people, on the right platforms, at the right times.

Key AI Tools for Content Distribution:

- **Buffer's AI Assistant**: Analyzes your audience engagement patterns across platforms to recommend optimal posting times and content formats.
- **Hootsuite Insights**: Uses AI to track conversations around your industry and identify opportunities to join discussions with your content.
- **Missinglettr**: Automatically creates year-long social media campaigns from each piece of content you publish, using AI to extract key quotes and create platform-specific posts.
- **Repurpose.io**: Uses AI to transform your primary content (like a podcast or video) into multiple formats for different platforms.
- **CopyAI**: Generates platform-specific variations of your content with appropriate hooks, hashtags, and calls to action.

Practical Application Strategy:

1. Create your primary content in your strongest format (writing, video, audio).
2. Use Repurpose.io to transform it into multiple formats.
3. Use CopyAI to craft platform-specific messaging for each piece.
4. Schedule distribution using Buffer's AI recommendations for timing.

5. Use Hootsuite Insights to identify conversations where you can share your content as a valuable contribution.

4. Audience Engagement: Building Relationships at Scale

Building an audience isn't just about broadcasting—it's about fostering relationships. AI tools can help you engage authentically with more people than would otherwise be humanly possible.

Key AI Tools for Audience Engagement:

- **Levity**: Uses AI to categorize and prioritize comments and messages across platforms so you can focus on the most meaningful interactions.
- **Respondable**: Analyzes your email and message responses in real-time to ensure they strike the right tone and are likely to receive a positive response.
- **Polymer**: Creates personalized video responses at scale by using AI to identify common questions and generate custom video scripts.
- **Typewise**: Offers advanced AI-powered text prediction that learns your unique communication style, making responses faster and more authentic.
- **Phrasee**: Uses AI to optimize your subject lines and opening sentences for better engagement rates.

Practical Application Strategy:

1. Use Levity to identify patterns in audience questions and comments.
2. Create templated responses to common questions in your authentic voice.
3. Use Respondable to ensure your responses maintain the right tone.
4. For high-value connections, use Polymer to create personalized video responses.

The Content Flywheel: Building Momentum with AI

The true power of AI in audience building comes from creating a self-reinforcing content flywheel, where each piece of content informs and enhances the next.

Here's how to build your AI-powered content flywheel:

1. **Create** foundational content using AI writing assistants
2. **Analyze** performance with AI analytics tools
3. **Refine** your approach based on data insights
4. **Expand** successful content into multiple formats
5. **Distribute** across platforms using AI scheduling and optimization
6. **Engage** with your audience using AI prioritization
7. **Learn** from engagement to inform new content
8. **Repeat** with increasingly refined strategy

As your flywheel gains momentum, the effort required to maintain and grow your audience diminishes while the results compound.

The Five-Week Audience Building Sprint

Building an audience can feel overwhelming, but it becomes manageable when broken down into a structured sprint. Here's a five-week plan to leverage AI for audience building:

Week 1: Foundation Setting

- Use MarketMuse or BuzzSumo to identify your unique content niche
- Create your audience persona with AI assistance
- Set up content repositories and workflows
- Choose your primary and secondary platforms

Week 2: Content Creation

- Produce 3-5 pieces of foundational content with AI assistance
- Focus on quality rather than quantity

- Develop a consistent style and voice
- Create content templates for future use

Week 3: Distribution Setup

- Set up Missinglettr and Buffer accounts
- Create platform-specific messaging for your content
- Build a distribution calendar
- Implement tracking links for performance analysis

Week 4: Engagement Systems

- Create response templates for common interactions
- Set up notification systems with priority filters
- Establish a daily engagement routine
- Create a feedback collection system

Week 5: Analysis and Optimization

- Review performance data from all platforms
- Identify high-performing content and formats
- Refine your strategy based on insights
- Set up automated reporting systems

This sprint approach gives you a functional audience-building system in just over a month. From there, it's about iteration and improvement rather than starting from scratch.

Ethical Considerations in AI-Enhanced Audience Building

As you leverage AI to build your audience, certain ethical considerations deserve attention:

1. **Authenticity**: Use AI to amplify your voice, not replace it. Your audience connects with you, not an algorithm.
2. **Transparency**: Be open about your use of AI tools. Today's audiences appreciate behind-the-scenes insights into your process.

3. **Value delivery**: Focus on using AI to deliver more value to your audience, not just to produce more content.
4. **Responsible scaling**: As you grow, maintain the personal touch that made people connect with you in the first place.

Measuring Success: Beyond Vanity Metrics

Building an audience isn't about accumulating followers—it's about creating meaningful connections that translate into opportunities. Focus on these metrics:

- **Engagement rate**: The percentage of your audience that interacts with your content
- **Content resonance**: How long people engage with your content
- **Conversion metrics**: Actions taken as a result of engagement (newsletter signups, consultations, etc.)
- **Opportunity pipeline**: Direct opportunities that come from your audience-building efforts
- **Network growth**: Quality connections added to your professional network

A software developer with just 2,000 LinkedIn followers generated more client inquiries than a competitor with 50,000 followers because they focused on engagement and conversion rather than follower count.

Common Pitfalls and How to Avoid Them

As you build your audience with AI assistance, watch for these common pitfalls:

1. **Content without perspective**: AI can generate bland, generic content. Always infuse your unique insights and experiences.
2. **Platform addiction**: Spreading yourself too thin across multiple platforms dilutes your impact. Start with one primary platform.
3. **Automation overreliance**: Automated systems should enhance personal connection, not replace it.
4. **Metric fixation**: Don't let metrics drive your strategy at the expense of authentic connection.

5. **Inconsistency**: The number one killer of audience growth is inconsistent presence. Use AI to maintain consistency even when your schedule gets busy.

The Future of Audience Building: AI as Your Creative Partner

As AI continues to evolve, the relationship between creators and their AI tools will become increasingly collaborative. Future AI audience-building tools will:

- Predict content trends before they emerge
- Generate personalized content recommendations for each audience segment
- Create interactive content experiences that adapt to user engagement
- Facilitate more natural, conversational engagement at scale
- Integrate virtual and augmented reality elements into your content strategy

The creators who thrive will be those who view AI not as a replacement for human creativity, but as a powerful amplifier of it—a creative partner that handles routine tasks while freeing you to focus on the uniquely human elements of connection and insight.

Conclusion: Your Unfair Advantage

In the AI era, your ability to build and nurture an audience is perhaps your greatest professional asset. While credentials, skills, and experience remain important, your audience represents something far more valuable: a direct channel to opportunity that no algorithm can disrupt.

By leveraging AI tools strategically across the four pillars of audience building—content creation, strategy, distribution, and engagement—you create a resilient professional presence that grows in value over time.

The true power of AI in audience building isn't that it does the work for you, but that it eliminates the busywork that previously prevented great ideas from reaching the people who needed them most. In doing so, it democratizes influence in ways that were unimaginable just a few years ago.

The question is no longer whether you can afford to invest in building an audience, but whether you can afford not to. In a world where AI is disrupting traditional career paths daily, your audience isn't just a nice-to-have—it's your professional insurance policy, opportunity generator, and legacy all in one.

The tools are available. The strategies are proven. The only remaining ingredient is your commitment to sharing your unique perspective with the world.

Chapter 8: The Force Multiplier: How to Combine AI Powers for Exponential Results

In the emerging landscape of AI capabilities, the true winners won't be those who master a single AI tool or skill, but those who learn to combine multiple AI powers in synergistic ways. This chapter explores how the convergence of building, automating, creating, and connecting capabilities creates exponential rather than merely additive results.

The Synergy Principle

When you combine different AI powers, you don't just add their benefits—you multiply them. This is similar to how different instruments in an orchestra create music that's far more powerful than each instrument playing separately. The whole truly becomes greater than the sum of its parts.

Consider what happens when you combine:

- Building + Automating = Self-improving systems
- Creating + Connecting = Audience-building engines
- Building + Creating = Custom content factories
- Automating + Connecting = Personal brand amplifiers

Let's explore practical workflows that demonstrate this synergy in action, with specific tools and techniques you can implement immediately.

Building + Automating: Self-Improving Systems

When you combine the power to build software with the power to automate processes, you create systems that can evolve and improve with minimal supervision.

Example Workflow: Customer Feedback Loop

1. **Build a feedback collection app** using Bolt or Repl.it Agent where customers can share their experiences

2. **Automate analysis** using Zapier to send this feedback to Claude or GPT
3. **Generate insights** that automatically update your product dashboard
4. **Trigger improvements** based on patterns detected in the feedback

Tools to Combine:

- Repl.it Agent for building the feedback interface
- Make.com for creating the workflow automation
- OpenAI's API for processing and analyzing feedback
- Relevance AI for categorizing and prioritizing feedback

By combining these tools, you create a system that continuously collects insights and uses them to improve your products or services without constant manual intervention.

Creating + Connecting: Audience-Building Engines

The combination of content creation and audience building creates a powerful engine for influence and growth.

Example Workflow: Content Ecosystem

1. **Create cornerstone content** using AI writing assistants to develop comprehensive guides
2. **Generate derivative pieces** with Midjourney and DALL-E for visuals and Claude for repurposing
3. **Establish automated distribution** through multiple channels
4. **Engage with audience responses** using AI to help personalize interactions

Tools to Combine:

- Claude for writing long-form content
- Midjourney for creating supporting visuals
- Runway AI for short-form video variations
- Zapier for scheduling and cross-posting

- Sona for creating original audio versions

Someone implementing this approach can build an audience across multiple platforms while only creating core ideas once. The system handles transforming content for different mediums and platforms.

Building + Creating: Custom Content Factories

Combining software building with content creation capabilities allows you to create specialized tools that produce exactly the content you need.

Example Workflow: Customized Educational Materials

1. **Build a content specification tool** using Repl.it Agent
2. **Feed specifications** to various AI creative tools
3. **Generate customized educational materials** tailored to specific learners
4. **Track engagement and results** to improve future iterations

Tools to Combine:

- Bolt for building the customization interface
- Claude for generating educational text
- Synthesia for creating instructional videos
- DALL-E for creating educational illustrations
- Descript for polishing final audio/video outputs

A teacher or educational content creator can generate dozens of variations of learning materials targeted to different learning styles, all from a single input specification.

Automating + Connecting: Personal Brand Amplifiers

When you combine automation with connection capabilities, you can dramatically extend your reach and influence with minimal additional effort.

Example Workflow: Multi-Channel Thought Leadership

1. **Create core insights** using AI writing tools
2. **Automate transformations** into multiple formats
3. **Distribute across platforms** with personalized timing and formatting
4. **Engage with responses** using AI assistance

Tools to Combine:

- Claude for developing core ideas and perspectives
- Zapier for triggering content variations
- DALL-E for generating supporting images
- Synthesia for creating video versions
- Postman for connecting to various platform APIs

A thought leader or industry expert can share insights once and have them automatically transformed and distributed across multiple platforms, dramatically increasing visibility with minimal additional effort.

Building + Creating + Automating: End-to-End Product Development

Adding a third power creates even more powerful combinations. By combining building, creating, and automating, you can develop complete products with minimal resources.

Example Workflow: Digital Product Creation

1. **Build a product creation tool** using Repl.it Agent
2. **Generate product components** using AI creative tools
3. **Automate assembly and distribution** of the final product
4. **Collect feedback and iterate** automatically

Tools to Combine:

- Bolt for building the product interface
- Midjourney for generating product visuals
- Claude for creating product documentation
- Zapier for handling product delivery
- Relevance AI for processing customer feedback

A solo entrepreneur can create, refine, and distribute digital products at a pace that previously required entire teams.

Automating + Connecting + Creating: Content Personalization at Scale

By combining three powers, you can create sophisticated content systems that adapt to individual audience members.

Example Workflow: Personalized Learning Experiences

1. **Automate learner data collection** through various touchpoints
2. **Create custom learning paths** based on individual needs
3. **Generate personalized content** for each learner
4. **Build connections** through tailored engagement

Tools to Combine:

- Make.com for creating the learner profile workflows
- Claude for developing personalized learning plans
- DALL-E for generating custom illustrations
- Descript for creating custom audio explanations
- Zapier for delivering content at optimal times

An educator or course creator can provide thousands of students with learning experiences that feel individually crafted without manually creating each variation.

Building + Automating + Connecting + Creating: The Ultimate Force Multiplier

When you combine all four powers, you become capable of accomplishments that would normally require entire organizations.

Example Workflow: Complete Business Ecosystem

1. **Build your business infrastructure** using AI development tools
2. **Create all necessary content assets** using AI creative tools
3. **Automate core business processes** using AI agents and workflows

4. **Connect with customers and partners** through AI-enhanced communications

Tools to Combine:

- Repl.it Agent for building business applications
- Claude and DALL-E for creating marketing materials
- OpenAI's GPTs for creating specialized business agents
- Zapier and Make.com for business process automation
- Runway AI for customer-facing video content

A solo entrepreneur can operate at the scale of a small company by effectively leveraging all four AI powers in concert.

Practical Integration Strategies

Combining AI powers effectively requires thoughtful planning and integration. Here are key strategies to maximize your results:

1. Start with Clear Workflows

Before combining tools, map out complete workflows from input to final output. Identify:

- Where data needs to flow between systems
- Potential bottlenecks
- Manual steps that could be eliminated

For example, if you're creating content, map the flow from idea generation to publishing and promotion, identifying every transition point.

2. Use API Connections Where Possible

Direct API connections between tools create more reliable and efficient workflows than manual transfers.

Tools like Postman make it easier to understand and implement these connections, even without advanced programming knowledge. For instance, connecting Midjourney outputs directly to your content management system eliminates manual downloading and uploading.

3. Implement Middleware When Needed

Sometimes tools don't connect directly. In these cases, middleware solutions can bridge the gap:

- Zapier and Make.com for general automation
- n8n for more complex, self-hosted workflows
- Custom webhooks created with Repl.it Agent

For example, if you need to move data between a custom tool and a social media platform, a middleware solution can handle the translation and formatting.

4. Create Feedback Loops

The most powerful combined systems include feedback mechanisms that use results to improve future iterations.

For example, a content creation system might:

- Track engagement metrics for published content
- Feed those metrics back to content planning tools
- Automatically adjust future content based on what resonated

5. Document Your Systems

As your combined workflows grow more complex, documentation becomes essential:

- Record the purpose of each connection
- Document the data format at each transition point
- Create troubleshooting guides for common issues

Tools like Notion with Claude integration can help maintain living documentation that evolves with your systems.

Overcoming Common Integration Challenges

Combining AI powers often presents challenges. Here are solutions to typical obstacles:

Challenge: Data Format Inconsistencies

Different AI tools often use different data formats, creating compatibility issues.

Solution: Implement format conversion steps in your workflow. Tools like Make.com excel at transforming data between formats. For example, you might need to convert JSON outputs from one API into CSV format for another.

Challenge: Rate Limits and Quota Constraints

Many AI tools impose usage limits that can disrupt complex workflows.

Solution: Implement queuing systems and retry logic in your automations. Tools like n8n offer robust handling of rate limits, allowing your workflows to pause and resume rather than fail when limits are reached.

Challenge: Maintaining Quality Across Transitions

Quality can degrade as content or data moves between different AI systems.

Solution: Implement quality checkpoints at key transition points. These might be automated checks using Claude to evaluate outputs, or strategic human review steps for critical transitions.

Challenge: Keeping Systems in Sync

As tools update and evolve, previously working integrations may break.

Solution: Build monitoring into your systems that alerts you to failures or anomalies. Tools like Zapier's status alerts can notify you when workflows fail, allowing for quick intervention.

Case Studies in Power Combination

Let's explore some practical implementations of combined AI powers:

Educational Content Creation System

An educator could combine:

- Building: A custom specification tool for lesson requirements
- Creating: AI generation of text, images, and videos for lessons
- Automating: Workflows for assembling materials into complete lessons
- Connecting: Systems for distributing materials to students and collecting feedback

Key tools would include Repl.it Agent for the specification interface, Claude for text generation, DALL-E for visuals, Descript for video, and Zapier for orchestration.

Customer Service Enhancement

A small business could combine:

- Building: A custom customer interaction portal
- Automating: AI agents to handle routine inquiries
- Creating: Personalized response templates for complex situations
- Connecting: Follow-up systems that strengthen customer relationships

This would use tools like Bolt for the portal, OpenAI's GPTs for the agents, Claude for response templates, and Make.com for the follow-up systems.

Product Development Ecosystem

A product creator could combine:

- Building: Tools for product specification and testing
- Creating: Design assets and marketing materials
- Automating: Production and distribution workflows
- Connecting: Customer feedback and improvement systems

This might use Repl.it Agent for specification tools, Midjourney for design, Zapier for workflows, and Claude for processing feedback.

Future-Proofing Your Combined Powers

The AI landscape evolves rapidly. To ensure your combined systems remain effective:

1. Modular Design

Build your integrations with modular components that can be replaced as better tools emerge. Avoid deep dependencies on any single tool's proprietary features.

2. Regular Capability Audits

Schedule quarterly reviews of new AI tools and capabilities. Assess whether emerging tools offer significant improvements over your current solutions.

3. Continuous Learning

Set aside time to experiment with new integration possibilities. The intersection of emerging tools often creates the most powerful new capabilities.

4. Community Engagement

Participate in communities where others are combining AI powers in similar ways. Platforms like Discord servers for specific tools often share integration techniques and solutions.

Conclusion: The Exponential Advantage

As we move further into the AI age, the gap will widen between those who use AI tools in isolation and those who combine them into integrated systems. The difference isn't just quantitative—it's qualitative, transforming what's possible for individuals and small teams.

By thoughtfully combining the powers of building, automating, creating, and connecting, you position yourself to achieve results that would previously have required significant resources and specialized teams. You become the force multiplier—the individual whose capabilities are exponentially expanded through the strategic combination of AI powers.

The future belongs not just to those who master individual AI tools, but to those who orchestrate these tools into symphonies of capability that transform their work, creativity, and impact.

Chapter 9: Zero to Hero: The 90-Day Roadmap to AI Mastery

Becoming an AI generalist doesn't happen overnight, but with a structured approach, you can master the essential skills in just 90 days. This roadmap divides your journey into three 30-day phases, each building upon the previous one to transform you from a beginner to a capable AI generalist ready to thrive in the new economy.

Phase 1: Building Your Foundation (Days 1-30)

Week 1-2: Understanding AI Fundamentals

Begin by developing a basic understanding of how AI works without getting lost in technical complexities. Focus on:

- **Learning the core concepts**: Spend time with beginner-friendly resources like AI For Everyone (Coursera) or the Elements of AI free online course.
- **Understanding prompt engineering basics**: Practice crafting effective prompts using Claude, ChatGPT, or Bard. Start with simple tasks like asking for summaries or explanations.
- **Exploring AI capabilities**: Test different types of requests to understand what AI can and cannot do effectively.

Practical Exercise: Create a personal AI assistant using ChatGPT or Claude to help with daily tasks like drafting emails, summarizing articles, or planning schedules.

Week 3-4: Mastering AI-Enhanced Writing

Develop your first power: the ability to communicate effectively with AI assistance.

- **Learn structured prompting**: Practice using frameworks like CRISPE (Context, Request, Instructions, Specifications, Persona, Examples) to get more precise outputs.

- **Develop content creation workflows**: Use tools like Notion AI, ClickUp AI, or Jasper to draft blog posts, social media content, or reports.
- **Edit and refine with AI**: Learn to use Claude or GPT-4 to improve your existing writing, not just generate new content.

Practical Exercise: Create a content calendar for a hypothetical business or personal project, then use AI to draft five different pieces of content following that plan.

Phase 2: Expanding Your Capabilities (Days 31-60)

Week 5-6: Building Without Coding

Develop your second power: creating software without traditional programming skills.

- **Learn AI-assisted development**: Start with user-friendly tools like Replit, Bolt, or GPT-4 to generate simple code from descriptions.
- **Create a simple web application**: Use platforms like Bubble or Webflow with AI integration to build a functional website or app.
- **Implement basic automations**: Learn to connect services using Zapier or Make to automate simple workflows.

Practical Exercise: Build a simple tool that solves a specific problem you face. This could be a custom calculator, a data visualization dashboard, or a form that processes information in a unique way.

Week 7-8: Generating Professional Content

Develop your third power: creating professional-grade content across multiple media formats.

- **Master image generation**: Learn to use Midjourney, DALL-E, or Stability AI to create custom visuals based on detailed prompts.
- **Explore AI video creation**: Experiment with tools like Runway, Synthesia, or Descript to create and edit video content.
- **Generate audio content**: Use tools like ElevenLabs, Descript, or Resemble.ai to create voiceovers and audio elements.

Practical Exercise: Create a multimedia presentation or pitch deck that incorporates AI-generated images, charts, and potentially video elements or animations.

Phase 3: Becoming an AI Powerhouse (Days 61-90)

Week 9-10: Building Your AI Workforce

Develop your fourth power: creating AI agents and automations that work for you.

- **Design AI agents**: Use platforms like AutoGPT, Relevance AI, or custom GPTs to create specialized agents that perform specific tasks.
- **Create advanced workflows**: Build multi-step automations that connect various tools and services using Make, Zapier, or n8n.
- **Implement feedback loops**: Learn to create systems where outputs from one step become inputs for another.

Practical Exercise: Create an automated research system that collects information on a topic of interest, summarizes findings, and generates insights or recommendations.

Week 11-12: Integration and Optimization

Learn to combine all four powers for exponential results.

- **Build integrated systems**: Connect your AI tools and workflows to create end-to-end solutions.
- **Optimize for efficiency**: Refine your prompts and workflows to reduce costs and improve output quality.
- **Develop quality control processes**: Implement checks and reviews to ensure AI outputs meet your standards.

Practical Exercise: Create a comprehensive project that utilizes all four AI powers: build a simple tool, automate its operation, generate content to explain it, and develop a plan to share it with others.

Daily Practices Throughout the 90 Days

To maximize your progress, incorporate these daily habits:

1. **20-minute skill building**: Dedicate at least 20 minutes daily to learning a specific AI tool or technique.
2. **Problem-solving practice**: Identify one regular task and attempt to solve it using AI tools.
3. **Reflection journal**: Document what worked, what didn't, and insights gained for future reference.
4. **Community engagement**: Participate in AI communities to learn from others and share your progress.

Essential Tools for Your AI Toolkit

AI-Enhanced Writing and Communication

- **Claude**: Exceptional for long-form content, creative writing, and detailed analysis
- **ChatGPT**: Versatile for various writing tasks and brainstorming
- **Google Gemini**: Strong for research-based writing and fact checking
- **Notion AI**: Integrated writing assistance within your knowledge management system
- **Grammarly**: Refines writing with grammar and style suggestions

Building Without Coding

- **Replit**: AI-assisted code generation and development environment
- **Bolt**: Create web applications through natural language descriptions
- **GPT-4 with Code Interpreter**: Generate and execute code to solve problems
- **Bubble**: No-code platform with AI capabilities for app development
- **Webflow**: Create professional websites with AI enhancement

Content Generation

- **Midjourney**: Generate highly artistic and detailed images

- **DALL-E**: Create diverse visual content from textual descriptions
- **Runway**: Produce and edit video content with AI
- **Descript**: Edit audio and video with text-based editing
- **ElevenLabs**: Generate natural-sounding voices for content
- **Canva with Magic Studio**: Create designs with AI assistance
- **Adobe Firefly**: Generate and edit creative assets ethically

Automation and AI Agents

- **Make (formerly Integromat)**: Build complex automated workflows
- **Zapier**: Connect applications and automate tasks
- **Relevance AI**: Create and deploy AI agents for specific purposes
- **AutoGPT**: Autonomous AI that can perform complex tasks
- **n8n**: Open-source workflow automation tool
- **Custom GPTs**: Create specialized AI assistants for specific domains

Overcoming Common Challenges

Challenge 1: Information Overload

- **Solution**: Focus on mastering one tool at a time rather than trying to learn everything at once. Start with versatile tools like Claude or ChatGPT that can help with multiple use cases.

Challenge 2: Unrealistic Expectations

- **Solution**: Understand that AI tools have limitations. Learn to recognize when AI is appropriate for a task and when human expertise is needed.

Challenge 3: Prompt Engineering Difficulties

- **Solution**: Use prompt templates and frameworks to structure your requests. Keep a library of successful prompts to reference and modify.

Challenge 4: Integration Complexity

- **Solution**: Start with simple connections between two tools before attempting complex workflows. Use established platforms like Zapier to simplify integration.

The Path Beyond 90 Days

After completing this roadmap, continue your journey by:

1. **Specializing in one power**: Dive deeper into the area that most interests you or benefits your work.
2. **Exploring emerging AI capabilities**: Stay current with new models and tools as they're released.
3. **Building a portfolio**: Document your projects to demonstrate your capabilities to potential employers or clients.
4. **Teaching others**: Solidify your knowledge by helping others learn these skills.

Remember that the goal isn't to replace human creativity or judgment but to augment your capabilities. The most successful AI generalists combine technological tools with critical thinking, ethical considerations, and a deep understanding of the problems they're trying to solve.

By following this roadmap consistently for 90 days, you'll develop a powerful set of skills that puts you ahead of the curve in the AI revolution. You'll be able to accomplish tasks that previously required teams of specialists, putting you in an excellent position to thrive in 2025 and beyond.

Chapter 10: Beyond 2030: Positioning Yourself for the Next Wave of AI Innovation

As we venture beyond 2030, the AI landscape continues to evolve at an unprecedented pace. The innovations that seemed revolutionary just a few years ago have become standard tools in our daily workflows. To stay relevant and thrive in this rapidly changing environment, you must develop a forward-thinking mindset and position yourself strategically for the next wave of AI innovation.

The Evolving AI Ecosystem

The AI revolution has moved far beyond the initial phase of automation and basic generative capabilities. The next frontier integrates several advanced technologies:

Autonomous AI Agents

AI agents have evolved from simple task executors to complex autonomous systems capable of managing entire workflows without human intervention. These agents now collaborate with each other, forming ecosystems that solve problems collectively.

Practical Application: AI orchestration platforms allow users to design systems where multiple specialized agents work together. A content creator might deploy a research agent that gathers information, feeds it to a writing agent, which then collaborates with a design agent to produce a complete multimedia package—all while the creator sleeps.

Multimodal Intelligence

The division between different forms of data—text, images, audio, video— has disappeared. Advanced AI systems process and generate across all modalities simultaneously, understanding the world more holistically.

Practical Application: Creative professionals use multimodal platforms that can take an idea expressed through voice, sketch, or text and instantly translate it across multiple forms. A filmmaker might describe a scene verbally, which the AI visualizes, scores with appropriate music, and even suggests dialogue that matches the emotional tone of the visuals.

Embodied AI

AI has moved beyond screens into the physical world through robotics and smart environments that sense, reason, and act in three-dimensional space.

Practical Application: Intuitive robotics platforms allow non-technical users to "train" physical systems through demonstration and natural language. A small business owner might show a robotic assistant how to arrange merchandise once, and the system learns to maintain the arrangement while adapting to new inventory.

Developing Future-Proof Skills

To thrive in the post-2030 landscape, certain capabilities will prove essential:

Systems Thinking

The ability to understand complex networks of AI tools and how they interact becomes more valuable than expertise with any single tool.

Practical Approach: Develop the habit of mapping relationships between different AI systems you use. Consider how outputs from one system might serve as inputs for another. Practice designing workflows that leverage multiple AI capabilities in sequence or parallel.

Cognitive Orchestration

The skill of directing and coordinating multiple AI systems toward unified goals becomes the new form of productivity.

Practical Application: Orchestration interfaces allow users to design intelligent workflows with simple drag-and-drop functionality. A researcher might create a system where one AI continuously monitors scientific journals, another evaluates findings for relevance, and a third generates insights that connect new discoveries to their specific work.

Ethical Guidance

As AI systems gain more autonomy, the ability to instill them with appropriate values and ensure they operate within ethical boundaries becomes crucial.

Practical Application: AI governance platforms enable users to define boundaries and principles that guide AI behavior. A healthcare provider might establish parameters ensuring patient privacy, medical accuracy, and compassionate communication across all their AI-powered systems.

Conceptual Prototyping

The capacity to rapidly develop and test ideas using AI tools accelerates innovation cycles dramatically.

Practical Application: Simulation environments allow entrepreneurs to test business concepts by modeling market conditions, customer behavior, and operational challenges before investing significant resources. A potential founder might explore dozens of business models in days rather than months.

Strategic Positioning

To capitalize on the next wave of AI innovation, consider these strategic approaches:

Transition from Tools to Ecosystems

Rather than focusing on mastering individual AI applications, develop expertise in designing ecosystems of complementary tools that amplify each other's capabilities.

Implementation Strategy: Begin building your personal AI stack—a collection of tools that work together seamlessly. Start with core functions like information processing, content creation, and decision support, then gradually add specialized tools that enhance your specific professional activities.

Cultivate Unique Data Streams

As generalized AI capabilities become ubiquitous, proprietary data and unique perspectives provide competitive differentiation.

Implementation Strategy: Develop systems for capturing valuable data in your domain. This might involve creating specialized sensors, establishing unique feedback mechanisms, or systematically documenting observations that others overlook. The insights derived from this proprietary data will distinguish your work from others using the same AI tools.

Focus on Human-AI Symbiosis

The most powerful applications emerge not when AI replaces human activities but when it amplifies distinctly human capabilities like creativity, empathy, and moral judgment.

Implementation Strategy: For each professional activity, ask not "How can AI do this for me?" but rather "How can AI enhance my human capabilities in this area?" Design workflows where AI handles analytical heavy lifting while you focus on adding uniquely human value through intuition, ethical consideration, and creative insight.

Build Meta-Skills Over Technical Proficiency

The specific technical skills needed for AI interaction change rapidly, but meta-skills endure.

Implementation Strategy: Invest time in developing adaptability, conceptual thinking, and learning how to learn. Practice working with unfamiliar AI systems regularly, focusing on quickly grasping fundamental principles rather than memorizing specific interfaces or commands.

Emerging Fields and Opportunities

Several domains are poised for transformation as AI continues to evolve:

Synthetic Biology and AI Integration

The convergence of AI with biological sciences creates unprecedented opportunities for innovation in healthcare, agriculture, and environmental sustainability.

Practical Application: Biological design platforms allow researchers to simulate genetic modifications and predict their effects with increasing accuracy. Scientists can rapidly prototype solutions to complex biological challenges, from disease treatment to crop resilience.

Augmented Cognition

Technologies that directly enhance human cognitive capabilities through AI-brain interfaces move from experimental to practical applications.

Practical Application: Cognitive enhancement tools help users overcome limitations in attention, memory, and processing speed. A student might use such tools to maintain focus during extended study sessions or to encode complex information more effectively in long-term memory.

Distributed Intelligence Networks

Collaborative systems where human and artificial intelligence work together across global networks tackle complex challenges beyond the reach of either alone.

Practical Application: Problem-solving platforms connect human experts with specialized AI systems to address multifaceted challenges. Environmental scientists might collaborate with community members and AI analysis tools to develop localized solutions for climate adaptation.

Experiential Creation

The ability to design immersive, personalized experiences becomes a central economic activity as virtual and augmented reality technologies mature.

Practical Application: Experience design tools enable creators to craft multi-sensory narratives that adapt to individual preferences and reactions. Entertainment professionals might develop stories that evolve based on the emotional responses of participants, creating deeply personalized experiences.

Practical Implementation Roadmap

To position yourself effectively for the post-2030 AI landscape, consider this progressive approach:

Phase 1: Exploration and Awareness

Begin by developing broad awareness of emerging AI capabilities across different domains. Subscribe to forward-looking AI research publications, participate in future-oriented professional communities, and regularly experiment with cutting-edge tools, even when they lack immediate practical application.

Phase 2: Strategic Experimentation

Identify areas where emerging AI capabilities intersect with your professional interests or personal passions. Allocate regular time for structured experimentation in these areas. Document your insights, focusing particularly on unexpected outcomes or limitations you discover.

Phase 3: Capability Building

Develop a systematic approach to building future-relevant capabilities. This might involve creating personal learning projects, seeking mentorship from those already working at the cutting edge, or participating in collaborative initiatives exploring new applications of AI technology.

Phase 4: Ecosystem Development

Begin cultivating a network of human and AI resources that complement your capabilities. This includes building relationships with others who possess complementary skills, assembling a custom toolkit of AI systems tailored to your specific needs, and developing processes for effectively coordinating these resources.

Phase 5: Adaptive Mastery

Reach a state where you can fluidly adapt to new AI developments, integrating them into your existing ecosystem while maintaining focus on your core objectives. At this stage, you're not just responding to technological change but actively shaping how new capabilities are applied in your domain.

Balancing Opportunity and Risk

The accelerating pace of AI development brings both unprecedented opportunities and significant challenges:

Technological Dependence

As AI systems become more integrated into our work and lives, the risk of unhealthy dependence increases.

Mitigation Strategy: Maintain proficiency in fundamental skills that underlie your field. Regularly practice working without AI assistance to ensure you retain core capabilities. Design deliberate periods of "AI fasting" where you rely entirely on your unaugmented abilities.

Cognitive Homogenization

Widespread use of similar AI systems could lead to standardized thinking patterns and reduced cognitive diversity.

Mitigation Strategy: Deliberately expose yourself to diverse perspectives and unconventional thinking. Seek out human collaborators from different backgrounds and disciplines. Configure your AI tools to prioritize unexpected or alternative approaches rather than consistently providing the most likely or popular solutions.

Security and Sovereignty

As AI systems gain more autonomy and access to sensitive information, questions of control and security become paramount.

Mitigation Strategy: Develop literacy in AI security practices. Implement graduated trust systems where AI autonomy increases only after demonstrating reliability. Create clear boundaries around data and decisions that remain under direct human control.

Future-Proofing Your Mindset

Beyond specific strategies and technologies, positioning yourself for the next wave of AI innovation requires cultivating certain mental habits:

Embracing Productive Uncertainty

The most significant opportunities often emerge from areas of uncertainty and rapid change. Developing comfort with ambiguity and provisional knowledge becomes essential.

Practical Approach: Practice working with incomplete information and revising your understanding as new data emerges. Treat initial failures or unexpected outcomes as valuable intelligence rather than setbacks. Develop the habit of holding multiple, sometimes contradictory, hypotheses simultaneously.

Balancing Specialization and Adaptability

The tension between deep expertise and broad adaptability becomes increasingly important in the evolving AI landscape.

Practical Approach: Develop a "T-shaped" knowledge profile with depth in one area and breadth across many related domains. Allocate your learning time proportionally, with the majority focused on deepening your core expertise while regularly sampling adjacent fields and emerging technologies.

Cultivating Technological Intuition

The ability to develop intuitive understanding of new technologies—grasping their potential and limitations without exhaustive study—becomes increasingly valuable.

Practical Approach: When encountering new AI capabilities, focus first on understanding fundamental principles rather than implementation details. Develop the habit of asking "What makes this possible now that wasn't before?" and "What remains difficult despite this advancement?" Practice making predictions about how a technology might evolve, then follow up to see where your intuitions were accurate or misguided.

Conclusion

Positioning yourself for the AI landscape beyond 2030 isn't about predicting specific technological developments or mastering today's cutting-edge tools. Rather, it requires developing the adaptive capacity to thrive amid accelerating change. By cultivating a strategic mindset, building meta-skills that transcend particular technologies, and designing personal systems that enhance your unique human capabilities, you can do more than merely survive the next wave of AI innovation—you can help shape it.

The most successful individuals will be those who maintain a balanced perspective, seeing AI neither as a magical solution to all problems nor as a threat to human potential, but rather as a powerful set of capabilities that can amplify our distinctly human gifts. By approaching these technologies with curiosity, discernment, and a clear sense of purpose, you position yourself not just for professional success but for meaningful contribution in a world being transformed by artificial intelligence.